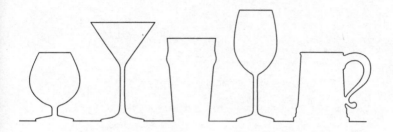

Guilt-Free Drinking

Why a diet including wine, beer and spirits in moderation
is *NOT* bad for your health

by

Robert Beardsmore

Vinifera Limited

ISBN 978-0-9566768-0-1

First published in Great Britain 2010
by Vinifera Limited

Acknowledgements

Like any other factual book, this book will probably not be entirely error free. Any errors or omissions are my responsibility and mine alone. However, this book is undoubtedly more accurate and better written for the constructive review and input of a number of people, to whom I am very grateful.

Particular thanks go to my brother, Dr John Beardsmore, and Dr Elizabeth Eaton for applying their medical scrutiny to the text, and to Laurie Edmond, who has spent many years in the area of biomedical research, for his numerous comments and suggestions. My parents and father-in-law, Stanley Peate, provided valuable feedback throughout the writing process. Dr Martin Hoyle and Geoff Taylor helped me clarify some technical points.

Finally, I am grateful to my wife, Rachael, for her patience and support in all aspects of this project; from listening to my early musings on the many research papers I read, all the way through to actually getting this book printed.

Acknowledgements

Contents

Preface

Have you ever had the feeling that something does not stack up? You have heard the arguments, the points of view, but you remain unconvinced. You are not an expert in the field so you cannot put your finger on the problem straight away, but you simply do not trust the conclusions that are being put before you. Your gut instinct is that all is not as it first appears. Your life experiences and broader knowledge lead you to the view that you are not being presented with the full picture.

Do you ever get the urge to investigate a subject for yourself, but you know you don't have the time? I am sure you have come across ideas and assertions that you would like to verify – and not just every time you hear a politician interviewed! There may be some truth in what you have read or heard, but it certainly is not the whole truth and nothing but the truth.

I felt this way about the myriad of negative reports relating to alcohol consumption. No-one doubts that alcohol can be abused, but is alcohol all bad? I decided to look into whether alcoholic beverages are as harmful as many maintain and discovered some fascinating facts.

1

Introduction

We have all heard of liver cirrhosis, even if we have to look it up in a dictionary to check how it is spelt. It is a serious and often fatal condition that is linked to a high consumption of alcohol. George Best is a tragic, high profile example of heavy drinking leading to cirrhosis of the liver and premature death. But most people do not drink like George Best.

Those that drink until their breath is almost flammable and then drive down the motorway at 100mph, will probably kill themselves. The greater tragedy would be the innocents wiped out at the same time during such an act of reckless lunacy. But most of us are not as irresponsible as that.

Getting drunk and having a fight on a Friday or Saturday night is a regular pastime for some. Alcohol induced fights and accidents represent a huge proportion of accident and emergency admissions at the weekend. But we don't have to frequent places where there are those that are out to get drunk and cause trouble.

If, like me, you don't drink yourself under the table, you don't drive recklessly and you are not into trouble-making, is drinking alcohol likely to do you harm? This should be at the heart of the debate around the consumption of alcoholic beverages. There are many nasties associated with drinking alcohol, but most are avoidable.

There is regular reporting of the scourge of anti-social behaviour. You cannot deny the link between alcohol and some anti-social behaviour. You cannot be drunk and disorderly without being drunk. But you can be drunk and not disorderly or disorderly without being drunk. The key ingredient in anti-social behaviour is not alcohol but attitude. As US President Abraham Lincoln put it so aptly over 200 years ago, "It has long been recognised that the problems with alcohol relate not to the use of a bad thing, but to the abuse of a good thing."

I think of wine, beer and spirits as elements of social conviviality. They help break the ice, de-stress the atmosphere and encourage mirth. With food, alcoholic beverages add to the enjoyment of the meal and assist in fostering a relaxing ambiance. At some social gatherings one might even concur with critic George J Nathan, who famously said, "I drink to make other people interesting."

From antiquity, alcoholic beverages have been an important part of people's diets. Wine in warmer climates and beer or cider in cooler climates were normal and substantial elements of everyday food and drink. No doubt wine and beer were safer than the water at many times in the past. Moreover, throughout recorded history, alcohol has been synonymous with weddings, feasting and celebrations that bring enjoyment across all strata of society. This connection between alcohol and positive social gatherings continues today.

But beyond alcohol's uplifting aspects, we all know that many older folk enjoy a few glasses of this or the odd tot of that and live to ages we would be quite happy to attain. And many doctors are not slow to recommend a few glasses of red wine to reduce the risk of heart problems.

A few years ago an acquaintance retired quite suddenly due to ill health. At his retirement party, he was asked by his work mates why he was leaving. He didn't want to be too explicit but did offer, "As well as giving up work, I'm going to have to give up the drink."

"All of it?" his colleagues replied, knowing how partial he was to a few glasses.

"Yes," he replied. "The doctor says I have to give up all alcohol …" and then he paused for a moment. "Except Doc says I can consume up to six bottles of red wine a week!"

This is only anecdotal, but you may have come across concepts such as the 'French paradox' that was much publicised in the early 1990s. This was the frequently used title given to the observation that despite the French having a diet high in saturated fat, their rate of coronary heart disease is low. This was put down to drinking large quantities of wine, particularly red wine.

So is it reasonable to classify alcohol as one of the major scourges of western civilizations? Should everyone be trying to drink less? Should governments be clamping down on all drinkers (that is most of us) through taxation and regulation? Do those that advocate abstention know what they are talking about? Should alcohol be classed alongside other harmful drugs such as nicotine or even with illegal drugs such as cocaine, cannabis and ecstasy? Should children be prevented from even taking a sip of an alcoholic drink? Should the minimum age for purchasing alcohol be increased? Should

there be health warnings on every bottle of booze? Should
we introduce prohibition?!

For the record, I am not an expert in any medical or
dietary field although I have always had an interest in nutrition. My formal training is in the areas of finance, IT and
management. Consequently, I have not conducted any health
studies of my own, but I have read hundreds of articles,
academic papers and summaries of papers on alcohol-related
studies and research together with voluminous reports
from governments and other policy-setting bodies. A very
substantial amount of research has been carried out into
the effects of consuming alcoholic beverages. In fact, the
quantity of research is staggering. That doesn't mean that
scientists and doctors know everything about drinking and its
effects on the body – far from it. Neither does it mean that
all the research gives the same conclusion. But it does mean
that there is a significant body of work from which one can
evaluate various claims about drinking.

This book does not try to show that alcoholic beverages
represent some kind of medicine that will cure the world's
ills. Nor does it attempt to paper over the issue of alcohol-
related harm. What I set out to investigate is whether those
of us that like to drink in moderation can do so without worrying that we may be damaging our health. In short, can we
drink without feeling guilty?

There is an aspect of all scientific research that is worthy of comment before starting to look at alcohol-related
research. Scientific research has a tendency to get politicised.
Either research grants are given out by bodies with a particular axe to grind, which may influence the way researchers

word their findings, or those summarising the research for the general populace or reporting it in the media apply their own slant. No-one can be totally free from bias. I recognise that that includes me. But please keep it in mind. I guess a rather poor pun here would be to say that depending on your starting point you may see a particular piece of research as showing that the glass is either half-full or half-empty.

For those of you that want to see the underlying research, footnotes are provided for many major studies and the appendix contains a short guide on how to access research papers and reports.

So where should we start in looking at how the benefits of consuming alcoholic beverages measure up against the evils that are constantly reported? We could start with heart disease. The effect of drinking on the risk of cardiovascular disease is one of the best researched areas. But we could look at the research that suggests benefits in relation to diabetes, osteoporosis, rheumatoid arthritis or even gall-stones. Or maybe we should look at the exciting research indicating benefits in staving off mental deterioration such as Alzheimer's disease?

We could, but we won't. I want to start with something that affects all of us: how long we live. In all health studies it is difficult to accurately isolate the exact effect of any aspect of diet because we are all eating and drinking many things other than the substance under investigation. We also subject our bodies to a wide range of other stresses and environmental factors. Moreover, with alcohol, it may well be that there is a mixture of benefits and disbenefits. If that is the case, we need to see whether there is a net gain from drinking.

One overarching measure of whether something is good for us or not is whether it helps us to live longer or knocks years off our lives. I won't keep you guessing; on average, drinking in moderation lengthens life.

2

Life and Death

It has long been recognised that drinking can have some health benefits. For example, an old Russian proverb says, "Drink a glass of wine after your soup and you steal a rouble from the doctor." However, although sayings such as this focus on positive aspects of drinking alcoholic beverages, we also know that consuming too much alcohol can cause terrible harm. Heavy drinking in Russia, particularly of their favourite vodka, has caused serious health problems. What we need to assess is whether moderate drinking is beneficial or deleterious to health.

Scientific studies have indicated a mixture of advantages and disadvantages to drinking, although most of the risks relate to heavier drinking. Some of these factors are large, others are marginal. In terms of saving lives, the most significant benefit is the reduction in cardiovascular disease, particularly a reduction in heart attacks. The areas of increased risk from drinking include specific cancers, such as in the liver and oesophagus, together with road and other accidents. We will look at these issues later in the book, but first we look at the overall balance.

Researchers around the world have set out to answer the question of whether drinking alcohol is likely to help us live

longer or not. Much of this epidemiological research takes
the form of prospective cohort studies. These studies typically select a large number of individuals and collect various
details from them. This may include age, sex, ethnicity, socio-
economic standing, current health, diet, etc and, of course,
data is collected on alcohol consumption. Records are then
kept on how many of these people die over a follow-up period that may vary from a few years to a number of decades.
From this data it is possible to estimate whether drinkers or
non-drinkers live longer on average. As this type of study is
simply looking at which groups live longer or shorter lives,
deaths from any cause are included in the statistics. The
results of these studies usually refer to 'all-cause mortality', in
other words death by any means. Studies looking at specific
diseases or causes of death will be more concerned about
the diagnosis of a particular ailment or cause of death, but
the one thing that can be said about all-cause mortality studies is that there is little room for error in determining which
category the participants end up in: at the conclusion of the
study, they are either in the land of the living or pushing up
the daisies.

In many studies, drinkers are also divided into a number
of categories such as light, moderate or heavy and data may
also include estimates of binge drinking. There are many
issues that affect how long we all live which is why data is
included on confounding issues. These are things that may
distort the data if they are not taken into consideration when
the statistics on mortality are calculated. An example would
be smoking. Smokers tend to die earlier than non-smokers
but there is also a strong correlation between heavy drinking

and smoking. If smoking is not addressed as a confounder in an alcohol study, the life expectancies of heavy drinkers might look worse than they really are because smoking is actually dragging down life expectancy. Heavy drinking smokers may die early, but it might not give a true reflection of life expectancy for heavy drinkers that do not smoke. Nobody can be sure that every issue has been considered, but many studies have now been carried out trying to get a clear picture of the effect of drinking alcoholic beverages whilst eliminating as far as possible other things that affect longevity.

No study on its own can give a perfect answer to this question on mortality and when governments set about creating public policy on alcohol they will review masses of epidemiological research in the area. Similarly, a number of researchers carry out meta-analyses, which are studies that try to pull together the numerous research papers from around the world to arrive at an answer that includes all the data available. These meta-analyses act as a useful summary of the research and by combining results create very large sample sizes. It is a core principle of statistics that the larger the number of people surveyed in a study, the more accurate the results are likely to be, so meta-analyses reduce statistical error in a similar way to large individual studies.

The first significant study of this kind was conducted in America by Raymond Pearl almost 90 years ago.[1] He delivered his findings in 1924, a period of some poignancy to anyone that likes a drink – particularly in the United States. It was 1920 that saw the introduction of the Volstead Act,

1   Pearl R. The influence of alcohol on duration of life. Proceedings of the National Academy of Sciences of the United States of America. June 1924; 10(6):231-7

which brought in prohibition together with the gangsters that flourished whilst alcohol was illegal. It is interesting to note that although American vineyards from 1920 until 1933, when the Act was repealed, were hardly profitable endeavours, the demand for table grapes and grape juice actually increased during the early years of prohibition. Although wineries could not make wine, they could still grow and sell grapes for winemaking at home. That remained legal!

Pearl's research was quite extensive, covering a group of over 6000 individuals all from comparable blue-collar backgrounds. He categorised individuals as abstainers, moderate drinkers or heavy drinkers. Abstainers had never used alcohol, moderate drinkers represented those whose alcohol intake was "never enough to become intoxicated" with heavy drinkers falling above that level. The definition of moderate drinker is quite generous, allowing a daily bottle of claret; not a major restriction for most, one would think.

In what seems rather a far-sighted detail when viewed in today's context of concern over heavy spates of drinking and binge drinking, Pearl also determined from his cohort the regularity of their drinking patterns.

From all this data Pearl calculated the life expectancy for men and women according to their ages from 30 years of age through to 100 years of age in 5-year intervals, categorised by drinking habit. His data showed that at all ages, moderate drinkers could expect longer life than abstainers. Sometimes the increase in longevity was quite modest and might not be considered statistically significant if the same research were carried out today. However, he also calculated the life expectancy of moderate drinkers who drank steadily, meaning most days. Their life expectancies were greater still than all the moderate drinkers, at all ages for women and up to age 65 for men. As might be expected, heavy drinkers tended to pop their clogs much sooner, particularly the women. Although heavy drinking men were always worse off than their moderate drinking colleagues, from age 65 they faired better than abstainers.

Presumably this evidence was not sufficient to persuade the prohibitionists, but it is an early example of a scientific investigation into the effects of alcohol on human health.

Fast forwarding eight decades, one of the largest meta-analyses to-date was carried out in 2006 with over a million people involved and over 94,500 deaths in the follow-up periods from 34 prospective studies carried out up to the end of 2005.[2] The sheer size of this analysis gives confidence that statistical margins of error will be small and a wide variation in study designs is covered. The overriding finding from this research was that mortality is indeed lower for moderate drinkers than abstainers with, as usual, heavy drinkers faring the worst. The same pattern applied to men and women although the upper level of drinking for women, at which there was no longer any benefit compared with abstainers, was about half that for men.

This research summarises much of the huge amount of effort that has gone into studying the effects of alcohol on all-cause mortality. In its detail there are differences not only between men and women but also between regions of the world. But despite these variations, the theme remains the

2   Di Castelnuovo A, Costanzo S, Bagnardi V, Donati M, Iacoviello L, de Gaetano G. Alcohol dosing and total mortality in men and women: an updated meta-analysis of 34 prospective studies. Archives of Internal Medicine. 11-25 Dec 2006; 166(22):2437-45.

same: moderate drinkers live longer than abstainers who in turn live longer than heavy drinkers.

That seems pretty clear. But let's take a slightly different angle on the subject. What do government experts think?

Governments are very coy about admitting that drinking alcohol is fine, let alone suggesting that it might actually be good for you. This contrasts with the many individual politicians that imbibe privately and publicly, and sometimes imbibe too much too publicly!

Understandably governments are concerned about saying something that might exacerbate the very real problems there are with those that do drink heavily. But, tucked away inside government reports they do have to acknowledge what the international research is saying.

In 1994 the British Government set up a working group to look at the evidence on the long-term effects of drinking alcohol. The working group included both medically and scientifically qualified members and generalists with relevant experience. It examined the major published research on alcohol drinking, received written evidence from academic and medical sources, the drinks industry and health promotion organisations, and called a number of experts to give oral evidence. The group's report was published under the title "Sensible Drinking" in December 1995 and remains the underpinning research for official UK guidelines on drinking.[3] The report is extremely thorough, covering all major aspects of the alcohol debate. This report states:

"Non drinkers have higher all-cause mortality than light and moderate

---

3   UK Department of Health. Safe. Sensible. Social. The next steps in the National Alcohol Strategy. 5 June 2007: p16

drinkers, and heavy drinkers have even higher all-cause mortality than either group." [4]

A similar statement appears in the 2005 Dietary Guidelines for Americans produced by the US Department of Health and Human Services and the US Department of Agriculture. It says:

"Alcohol may have beneficial effects when consumed in moderation. The lowest all-cause mortality occurs at an intake of one to two drinks per day. ... Morbidity and mortality are highest among those drinking large amounts of alcohol." [5]

The US guidelines provide a whole range of advice about diet and exercise. Nevertheless, in the section on alcohol, it recognises the potential benefits of drinking in moderation.

Finally, even the World Health Organization (WHO), which is at the forefront of trying to reduce alcohol consumption around the world, has some positive things to say. In the WHO Global Status Report on Alcohol 2004, it states:

"The most important health benefits of alcohol have been found in the area of coronary heart disease at low to moderate levels of average volume of alcohol consumption. Only a few individual-level studies have failed to substantiate this association in men or women." [6]

---

4   UK Department of Health. Sensible Drinking: The report of an inter-departmental working group. Dec 1995: p18. Reproduced under the terms of the Click-Use Licence.

5   U.S. Department of Health and Human Services and U.S. Department of Agriculture. Dietary Guidelines for Americans, 2005. 6th Edition, Washington, DC: U.S. Government Printing Office. January 2005: ch 9

6   World Health Organization. Global Status Report on Alcohol 2004: p41

This quote does not apply to all-cause mortality directly. The WHO report is a global report dealing with developing countries as well as the developed world. There tends to be less coronary heart disease in developing countries so a benefit of drinking alcohol in this area of health may not be so important. However, because coronary heart disease is such a big killer in developed countries, the reduction in deaths in this area tends to lead to a lower overall mortality for moderate drinkers in the western world.

There it is. Scientific research, governments and the WHO explicitly or implicitly recognise the overall benefit of moderate drinking. Of course, there are many issues still to consider. What level of drinking is moderate? Is it the same for all ages? Does it matter what we drink? We have already had brief indications that the pattern of drinking might be important and that moderate probably does not mean the same thing for women as it does for men. Then there is the issue of specific diseases. We may be better off drinking overall, but are there negatives that partly offset the positives?

Nevertheless, on average, drinking in moderation increases longevity.

So with scientific research, governments and the WHO demonstrating that moderate alcohol consumption is beneficial to overall longevity you might think the main argument is done and dusted. Not quite. Read on.

3

A Fly in Your Drink

Unfortunately, research into nutrition is rarely cut and dried. We humans are just too complicated. We all lead different lives, have different genes, consume different cocktails of food and drink. Some of us smoke; some of us don't. Some of us exercise; some of us don't. Some of us are fat; some of us are skin and bone. Some of us are innately upbeat; some of us are miserable. On top of that, or possibly because of it, some of us drink alcohol and some of us don't.

For researchers, it makes it very difficult to say with certainty that drinking alcohol, and drinking alcohol alone, does this or that. Research may point in a particular direction but 100% proof is in short supply.

It is a bit like the difference between a civil and criminal trial. In a civil court, the verdict is based on the preponderance of the evidence; in other words, the more convincing evidence wins the case. In a civil trial, relying on current research, one could win the case that moderate drinking increases longevity.

In a criminal trial, the case has to be made beyond a reasonable doubt. Here it gets a bit more tricky. With something as complex as the human body, can one say that moderate drinking is definitely good for you? I think the jury might be shut away in deliberations for a number of hours on that one. The case would be put to them that the research done to-date, although extensive, still falls short of absolute proof. Could there be another factor that is actually causing the apparent benefit that has nothing to do with alcohol at all? Or could it be that there is some systemic error that pervades the research?

The alcohol doubters will use all those arguments and, in fairness, doubters should not be discouraged. In true scientific debate, theories, even well established ones, should be open to challenge. Take for instance the current scientific theory of global warming being produced by man-made carbon dioxide. Here, unfortunately, anyone who tries to view the issue from a non-consensus perspective or suggests alternative contributing factors is deemed a scientific heretic. Regardless of your personal views on a scientific subject, diverse theories should be tested to help separate fact from hypothesis. John Beddington, chief scientific adviser to the British Government and supporter of the consensus view on climate change, recently commented, "I don't think it's healthy to dismiss proper scepticism. Science grows and improves in the light of criticism."[1] Bear in mind that less than 40 years ago, Newsweek ran an article entitled "The Cooling World"[2] commenting on the massive accumulation of evidence in support of global cooling. Just because a theory is popular at a particular point in time, does not make it an inviolable truth. Like lapel sizes and skirt lengths, scientific theories can go through fashions.

---

1   "John Beddington: chief scientist says climate change sceptics 'should not be dismissed'". Telegraph.co.uk. 27 January 2010

2   Newsweek. 28 April 1975: p64

Epidemiological research can shine a light on many health issues, but it can never illuminate every nook and cranny; there will always be remaining doubts or conundrums. Writing about the problems with epidemiological studies, A R Feinstein made the observation that, "The people who struggle to understand those [epidemiological] results can be helped by recalling the old adage that statistics are like a bikini bathing suit: what is revealed is interesting; what is concealed is crucial."[3]

So what are the potential flaws in the scientific studies that show that moderate drinking is good for longevity? The major criticism is about the way some of the research was formulated. In most of these studies, abstainers are used as the benchmark group for determining whether drinking extends or reduces life. It was in the late 1980s that The Lancet published a paper by Shaper et al that raised the concern that this abstainer group may not be a good benchmark.[4] The hypothesis was put forward that if the abstainer group contained many ex-drinkers, who had given up alcohol due to ill health, this group would look artificially sickly compared with those that are still drinking. Or, put the other way around, drinkers would look healthier than abstainers, but this could have nothing whatsoever to do with their drinking habits. These ex-drinkers became known as the 'sick quitters'.

Shaper and a number of other researchers around the world looked into the 'sick quitter' issue. By separating out ex-drinkers as a distinct group in mortality studies it became

---

3   Feinstein A. Scientific standards in epidemiological studies of the menace of daily life. Science. 3 Dec 1988; 242(4883):1257-63

4   Shaper A, Wannamethee G, Walker M. Alcohol and mortality in British men: explaining the U-shaped curve. The Lancet. 3 Dec 1988; 2(8623):1267-73

clear that they were not the sorts that life insurers would want on their books! This confirmed the view that abstainers were not a suitable benchmark group if ex-drinkers were included. The logical consequence of this was that the real benefit of drinking was probably rather less than the apparent benefits some of the earlier studies had shown.

With the ex-drinker issue taken on board, much of the ensuing research into mortality tried to make adjustments for this problem. Various techniques were used, but the main amendments were to exclude ex-drinkers from the abstainer group or to screen out those that already had known ill-health. The latter dealt with the ex-drinker problem as it is only those that stopped drinking because of ill-health that may distort the research. Sometimes these adjustments are difficult to achieve because many of these studies are conducted over long periods of time and it is not necessarily possible to ask new questions of participants where information on prior drinking or ill-health was not gathered at the beginning of the study. Many of the participants will have already drunk their last drink!

So what were the findings when 'sick quitters' were taken into account? Perhaps one good place to look is at further research carried out by Shaper and his colleagues. In 1994 they published the results of some research based on the British Regional Heart Study, which looked at total-mortality and the risk of coronary heart disease, where the majority of life-extending benefits are thought to lie. They reported that:

"Our own findings show that there is indeed a reduced relative risk of fatal CHD [coronary heart disease] events in men with no evidence of

pre-existing CHD who are moderate drinkers. However, in absolute terms, the reduced risk is small ... " [5]

The reduction in risk for those with pre-existing heart problems was actually greater. In relation to deaths from all causes, their report shows a small, not statistically significant, reduction in risk compared with their chosen benchmark group of occasional drinkers. It is worth mentioning that statistical significance is largely a function of the size of the sample; the larger the sample the smaller the margins of error and, hence, the more likely a result will be statistically significant. This report showed a number of benefits for drinkers, most of which were not statistically significant. However, it should also be noted that where the tables in the report indicated increased risks of death for heavy drinkers, none of these were statistically significant either.

In the "Sensible Drinking" report prepared for the British Government mentioned in the previous chapter, the authors had to consider whether alcohol was lowering the risk of death or whether, as Shaper suggested, the apparent benefit from drinking alcohol was merely a result of poorly designed studies that had not taken proper account of 'sick quitters'. They noted:

"...we believe Professor Shaper's reservations cannot be considered as a major explanation of the cardio-protective effect."

---

5   Shaper A, Wannamethee G, Walker M. Alcohol and coronary heart disease: a perspective from the British Regional Heart Study. International Journal of Epidemiology. Jun 1994; 23(3):482-94 by permission of Oxford University Press.

The report goes on to say:

"Other confounding factors such as tobacco use, obesity, diet and age have now been controlled for in enough studies to allow us, on the basis of expert testimony, to be confident that the basic protective effect for CHD [coronary heart disease] by alcohol is scientifically valid." [6]

So in many ways, focusing attention on the potential defects of some of the earlier research into the effects of alcohol on coronary heart disease, and hence longevity, has ensured that more robust research has been forthcoming. A number of studies have shown that the benefit of moderate drinking persists even when the abstainer group is more appropriately defined.[7,8,9]

The large meta-analysis mentioned in the previous chapter provides various statistics on the benefit provided by alcohol in reducing the risk of death from all causes.[10] As a meta-analysis, the report provides a summary of the many reports that make up the whole. One of the useful figures reported is the maximum benefit derived from drinking. This is achieved by looking for the greatest reduction in the risk of

6   UK Department of Health. Sensible Drinking: The report of an inter-departmental working group. Dec 1995: p8. Reproduced under the terms of the Click-Use Licence.

7   Thun M, Peto R, Lopez A, Monaco J, Henley S, Heath C Jr, Doll R. Alcohol consumption and mortality among middle-aged and elderly U.S. adults. The New England Journal of Medicine. 11 Dec 1997;337(24):1705-14.

8   Gmel G, Gutjahr E, Rehm J. How stable is the risk curve between alcohol and all-cause mortality and what factors influence the shape? A precision-weighted hierarchical meta-analysis. European Journal of Epidemiology. 2003; 18(7):631-42.

9   Doll R, Peto R, Boreham J, Sutherland I. Mortality in relation to alcohol consumption: a prospective study among male British doctors. International Journal of Epidemiology. Feb 2005; 34(1):199-204.

10   Di Castelnuovo A, Costanzo S, Bagnardi V, Donati M, Iacoviello L, de Gaetano G. Alcohol dosing and total mortality in men and women: an updated meta-analysis of 34 prospective studies. Archives of Internal Medicine. 11-25 Dec 2006; 166(22):2437-45.

death at any level of drinking from light through to heavy.

When all the results are combined, including a number of studies that have not been adjusted for the 'sick quitter' phenomenon, the maximum reduction in the risk of death from all causes is 19%. However, when the studies that included ex-drinkers in the benchmark abstainer group are removed, the maximum benefit falls to 16% with 99% confidence that the result lies between 14% and 18%. This again demonstrates that the 'sick quitter' issue is real but that after adjusting for this problem, a significant benefit for light to moderate alcohol drinkers remains.

More recently, another meta-analysis was carried out to look at the problems originally highlighted by Shaper. In this study, the researchers calculated relative risks of all-cause mortality for the few studies that they believed used an appropriate benchmark group of abstainers.[11] They concluded that there was no significant benefit to light and moderate drinkers in these few remaining studies. They did show small benefits for light and moderate drinkers but these were not statistically significant.

The same researchers published another paper in 2007 setting out further thoughts related to study design, again questioning the benefits of alcohol. So concerns over the real benefits of alcohol continue to be raised. Nevertheless, these researchers do explicitly conclude that alcohol conveys benefit to the heart,[12] but that the benefit has been

11   Fillmore K, Kerr W, Stockwell T, Chikritzhs T, Bostrom A. Moderate alcohol use and reduced mortality risk: systematic error in prospective studies. Addiction Research and Theory. Apr 2006; 14(2):101-32.

12   Fillmore K, Stockwell T, Chikritzhs T, Bostrom A, Kerr W. Moderate alcohol use and reduced mortality risk: systematic error in prospective studies and new hypotheses. Annals of Epidemiology. May 2007; 17(5 Suppl):S16-23.

exaggerated.

It would be incomplete to finish this chapter without mentioning that the benefit of alcohol for moderate drinkers could actually be greater than indicated by current research. Could it be that many heavy drinkers actually report that they are drinking moderately either through self-denial or because they are slightly embarrassed to admit to heavy drinking? In a recent report, researchers categorised roughly a quarter of moderate drinkers as "suspected under-reporters". When analysed as a separate group, they showed little of the benefits that moderate drinkers as a whole exhibited.[13] In other words, these under-reporters are making the genuine moderate drinkers look worse than they really are. If this is generally the case across studies, the benefits from moderate drinking are being undersold, not oversold!

So what can we conclude? There is little doubt that researchers should be very careful about defining their abstainer benchmark group. But what is the reality for drink-ers?

Most research still indicates an increase in longevity for moderate drinkers. We have seen that even Shaper, who as the inspiration behind the 'sick quitter' hypothesis was prob-ably one of the most stringent in defining abstainers, found small, albeit not statistically significant, benefits. And further, the recent meta-analysis based on Shaper's earlier work, whilst not supporting a beneficial effect of moderate drinking on longevity, found no negative consequence.

This seems positive news to me. The rigour of more recent studies has improved and yet most still support a ben-

13   Klatsky A, Udaltsova N. Alcohol drinking and total mortality risk. Annals of Epidemiology. 2007; 17:S63-7

eficial effect of moderate drinking. The worst case scenario is that there may be little or no benefit, but neither is it shortening your life. Heads you win, tails you get your money back!

4

Water of Life

Before looking in more detail at the longer-term effects of drinking, let us take a look at alcohol itself and how the body metabolises it. Potable alcohol is made by the natural process of fermentation; yeast converts sugar to ethanol, releasing carbon dioxide and heat. Nowadays, cultivated yeasts are often used for fermentation, but yeasts occur everywhere and will often start fermentations naturally if sugary solutions are left exposed to the air, for example in fruits where the skins have been broken. In traditional red winemaking, farm workers would tread out the grapes to break the skins and then the must would be put into open vessels to ferment. The yeasts that started the fermentation would be those occurring naturally on the skins of the grapes and, presumably, those occurring naturally on the feet and legs of those who had been squelching knee-deep in grape juice. Even in modern winemaking, winemakers rely on natural, often termed 'wild', yeasts to make some boutique wines. Producing wine this way is less controlled, but can give rise to wines with more complex flavours.

Years ago, distilled alcoholic beverages were often given the name *aqua vitae*, meaning water of life. This Latin term was translated into various languages as the basis of local names for distilled beverages. From France we have *eau de vie*, from Scandinavia *akvavit* and the names *whisky* and *whiskey* derive from the Gaelic *uisge-beatha* and the Irish *uisce beatha* respectively, all meaning water of life.

In the modern world, our names are more precise but rather less imaginative. There are a number of molecules in the alcohol family, but the one that we appreciate in our glass is ethanol. Ethanol is an organic molecule with the formula CH_3CH_2OH and is also known as ethyl alcohol, grain alcohol or just plain 'alcohol'. I will stick with 'alcohol' unless the context requires a more specific term. Alcoholic drinks do contain small amounts of other alcohols, but if they are present in anything more than limited quantities they can make you very ill.

In the UK, up to 9½ percent methanol is added to ethanol to make methylated spirits, which is poisonous. Other substances are added to give methylated spirits an unpleasant taste and odour, and it is also coloured with methyl violet to warn anyone from drinking it. Those that have become intoxicated on methylated spirits as a cheap substitute for potable alcohol sometimes pay the heavy price of going blind, caused by the methanol it contains. Longer chain alcohols, called fusel oils, are renowned for giving you a bad head-ache. In small quantities fusel oils can add to the character of some drinks, but generally, like methanol, they are far more toxic than ethanol. Fusel oils occur in small quantities in many alcoholic beverages as by-products of fermentation, but the most likely cause of high concentrations is poor distillation.

It is technically correct to say that ethanol is toxic as well.

However, one has to drink a substantial quantity of ethanol over a short period (and not vomit it up again!) to have much chance of getting ethanol poisoning. Unfortunately, every year, some people do manage to kill themselves this way.

Once alcohol enters the body, it requires no digestion. Alcohol is absorbed into the blood stream, slowly through the stomach and much more quickly through the small intestine. Approximately 90% of alcohol is metabolised in the liver. Most of the remainder is metabolised in the stomach or passes out of the body unchanged in breath, sweat and urine. Consequently, it is not surprising that the liver is one of the most likely organs to suffer damage in heavy drinkers.

One of the facts of drinking is that absorption of alcohol into the blood stream can occur much more quickly than the body, principally the liver, can metabolise it. The consequence of this is that unless we drink very slowly, the alcohol level in our blood increases. It is generally believed that the higher the blood alcohol concentration, or BAC, the more likely alcohol is to do damage to the body.[1]

In the liver, alcohol is broken down into acetaldehyde by the enzyme alcohol dehydrogenase. Acetaldehyde is then metabolised to acetate by the enzyme aldehyde dehydrogenase, which can then be further broken down to carbon dioxide and water. The rate at which this process occurs is close to constant, regardless of how much alcohol is in the blood that passes through the liver. A second metabolism route, with the lengthy description microsomal ethanol-oxidising system (MEOS), occurs in the liver using a different enzyme, P450. Regular drinkers, particularly heavier drinkers, build

---

1   Zakhari S. Overview: How is alcohol metabolized by the body? Alcohol Research & Health. 2006; 29(4):245-54

up a greater capacity to metabolise alcohol via this route. Although this might sound like a positive outcome, the break-down products from the MEOS pathway appear to magnify the risk of liver damage.[2] Consequently, regular heavier drinkers may be able to reduce their BAC more quickly than lighter drinkers, but the process is potentially more harmful to their livers.

A number of factors affect the BAC reached after drinking. Foremost is the amount of alcohol consumed and how quickly it is drunk. As the liver can only metabolise alcohol at a constant and relatively slow rate, rapid drinking leads to a high BAC. As mentioned above, regular drinkers may metabolise alcohol quicker via the more liver-damaging MEOS pathway.

The size, gender, fitness and age of the drinker have an effect on the BAC level. Alcohol is completely miscible with water and disperses throughout all the water in the various cells of the body, not just the blood. A bigger person has more water so the concentration of alcohol in the blood will be lower than for a smaller person, for the same quantity of alcohol consumed. Gender is important because it affects the proportion of water in the body. Alcohol does not penetrate fatty cells very much and women tend to have more adipose tissue than men. Consequently women have less body water in which to disperse the alcohol. On aver-age, 58% of a man's body is water compared with 49% for a woman.[3] Fitness and age are important because fitter people

---

2   Lieber C. Relationships between nutrition, alcohol use, and liver disease. *Alcohol Research & Health.* 2003; 27(3):220-31

3   National Highway Traffic Safety Administration, US. Computing a BAC Estimate. Oct 1994. No longer available from the NHTSA website, but a copy was accessed at www.stirlinglaw.com/phxcaa/issues/bac.htm on 4 February 2010

usually have more muscle, which has a high water content, and muscle bulk tends to decrease with age.

Drinking with food should lead to a lower BAC. The main reason is that although food does not absorb the alcohol, it does slow gastric emptying into the small intestine. This delayed release of food from the stomach also slows the release of alcohol from the stomach and hence moderates the rate of absorption of alcohol into the blood stream. A second benefit is that less alcohol may be spread around the body. Most alcohol is absorbed into the hepatic portal vein that delivers blood from around the gastrointestinal tract to the liver. If the rate of alcohol absorption is low, a greater percentage can be metabolised on its first time through the liver before it gets pumped around the rest of the body and dispersed into other body cells. This initial removal of alcohol from the blood is termed first pass metabolism. In addition, alcohol can be metabolised to some extent in the stomach by alcohol dehydrogenase, the same enzyme as in the liver. This is another form of first pass metabolism. The longer alcohol is held in the stomach the more alcohol (although still a relatively small proportion) can be metabolised without ever reaching the blood stream.[4] Therefore, the slower absorption of alcohol caused by food in the stomach gives the liver more time to metabolise the alcohol and moderate the rise in BAC, and additionally increases first pass metabolism that may prevent some alcohol from ever being dispersed around the cells of the body.

Some medicines can affect the absorption or metabolism

---

4   Oneta C, Simanowski U, Martinez M, Allali-Hassani A, Pares X, Homann N, Conradt C, Waldherr R, Fiehn W, Coutelle C, Seitz H. First pass metabolism of ethanol is strikingly influenced by the speed of gastric emptying. Gut. 1998;43:612-9

of alcohol and even carbon dioxide in your drink can make a difference. Fizzy alcoholic drinks are absorbed more quickly into your system than still drinks. Finally, as with all aspects of humans, there is genetic variability; in this instance people have different quantities of the various enzymes utilised in alcohol metabolism.

Alcohol's acute effects on the body can be largely described according to the BAC. The BAC can be quoted in various ways. For example, the legal driving limit in the UK is 80mg of alcohol per 100ml of blood; this is sometimes abbreviated to 80mg/100ml or shown as a percentage of 0.08.[5] The table opposite summarises the typical effects of increasing BAC.[6] Bear in mind that individual responses to alcohol can vary widely, so the table only gives a very rough guide to the progression of intoxication. At about 400mg/100ml, five times the legal drink-drive limit, the LD50 point is reached. LD50 stands for 'lethal dose, 50%' and represents the level of a toxin, here alcohol, that is expected to cause death in 50% of adults.

Due to all the issues outlined above that impact on BAC, it is difficult to give precise guidance on how much alcohol will lead to a potentially fatal BAC of 400mg of alcohol per 100ml of blood. However, in 1992, the National Highway Traffic Safety Administration in the US produced a method for estimating a BAC as part of a report to Congress on alcohol limits for drivers.[7] This same organisation's current

---

5   This is a rather strange percentage as the numerator is in grams and the denominator is in millilitres. Hence 80mg per 100ml becomes 0.08g/100ml or, ignoring units, 0.0008, which equals 0.08%.

6   Adapted from 'Chaves County DWI Program' – Effects of Alcohol Intoxication

7   The method of calculation is no longer available from the NHTSA website, but a copy was accessed at www.stirlinglaw.com/phxcaa/issues/bac.htm on 4 February 2010

BAC (mg/100ml)	Effects of BAC
Up to 60	Relaxation, lower inhibitions, minor impairment of reasoning and memory
60 – 100	Slight impairment of balance, speech, vision and reaction time. Reason and memory impaired. Euphoria.
100 – 150	Significant impairment of motor coordination, reaction time and judgement. Speech may be slurred and possible blurred vision.
150 – 300	Anxiety and possible nausea. May need assistance with walking. Mental confusion.
300 – 400	Loss of consciousness
Over 400	Potential onset of coma and death

stance is that no formula can accurately determine a BAC based on how much has been consumed because of individual and occasion specific variations. Although this is clearly correct, the formula they created, together with its many assumptions regarding average men and women, does give an indication of how intoxicated someone may get for a given intake of alcohol.

Using this method, a male weighing 12 stones (76kg) of average body composition would reach the LD50 blood alcohol concentration if he drank about a standard bottle of spirits (whisky, vodka, gin, rum, etc) in an hour. A petite woman weighing only 7 stones (45kg) would reach similarly serious intoxication drinking half a bottle of spirits in an hour.

Although I hope that reaching a lethal dose of alcohol

is, for most people, only a theoretical consideration, the varying BACs reached by different individuals after consuming the same amount of alcohol is an important factor for all of us. In particular, the difference between men and women is noteworthy. Women, on average, are smaller than men and contain less body water, so are likely to become more intoxicated than men for a given intake of alcohol. In addition, it is thought that women may have less ability to metabolise alcohol in the stomach,[8] meaning more alcohol reaches the blood stream.

Throughout the rest of this book, most analyses will be based on averages from various studies. Although this is useful for looking at populations as a whole, it is worth bearing in mind that no-one, actually, is average!

---

8   Mann R, Smart R, Govoni R. The epidemiology of alcoholic liver disease. Alcohol Research & Health. 2003;27(3):209-19

A Large Measure?

To understand the effects of drinking, we need to quantify how much pure alcohol is being consumed. For many of the benefits of drinking and almost all the downsides, the amount of alcohol being drunk is the important factor.

In olden days the concept of a 'proof spirit' was used to check that spirits such as brandy had not been watered down. A spirit was 'proven' if you could mix it with gunpowder and the whole lot would still go whoosh when you applied a flame to it. This threshold proportion of alcohol in the spirit was called 100% proof. Nowadays we measure alcohol by the proportion it represents in a drink, measured by volume. This measure is called 'alcohol by volume' or ABV, described on the label of all alcoholic beverages as 'x% ABV', or 'x% alc vol'. 100% proof is equivalent to just over 57% ABV.

Setting aside the general inaccessibility to gun powder these days, proving spirits was only any good for checking this 57% ABV threshold and the scale is not applied consistently in different countries. 100% proof may be 57% ABV in Britain, but in the United States the equivalent is about 114% proof. So for all practical purposes, everyone uses ABV.

Except scientists. They prefer to use grammes of alcohol. As alcohol weighs about 80% as much as water (actually, a specific gravity of 0.789) it is relatively easy to move between ABV and grammes. 100ml of alcohol equates to roughly 80g of alcohol.

But even that is not good enough for politicians and public health officials. They use standard drinks or units of alcohol. To be fair to politicians, something that requires great generosity of spirit, this is quite logical. Standard drinks or units allow comparison between different beverages. In the UK, one pub measure of spirits has roughly the same alcoholic content as half a pint of standard strength beer, with both equating to one unit of alcohol.

I say in the UK, because there is nothing consistent about these units or standard drinks around the world.[1] As a Brit, I hope the definition of our standard drink is not a measure of our hospitality. We use 8g of alcohol as a standard drink, the smallest measure anywhere in the world. As you might expect, the Irish measure is more generous at 10g. They are joined at 10g a unit by the antipodeans in Australia and New Zealand. Moving around Europe, the French, Austrians and Polish use 10g with The Netherlands shaving off a smidgen at 9.9g. The Italians use 12g as do the Danes. The Spanish cannot make their minds up and the Norwegians and Swedes don't care – or at least they haven't defined a standard drink, along with a number of other countries.

Move to North America and the Canadians use 13.6g only to be overtaken by the United States with 14g. But surely the greatest display of liberality is in Japan. There, if you are offered a standard drink you should be well pleased.

1   ICAP. International Drinking Guidelines.
www.icap.org/Table/InternationalDrinkingGuidelines

Consume two and you may start to feel inebriated. Down many more and you are probably on your way to quite a hangover. One Japanese standard drink is 19.75g of alcohol, equivalent to almost 2½ UK standard drinks. Japanese can be a difficult language for westerners to learn; perhaps something was lost in translation!

Anyway, as you can see, where alcohol is concerned there is little uniformity and we haven't even got to glass sizes yet. For the purposes of consistency, and hopefully not due to a lack of generosity, I will use 8g as the unit of alcohol, the UK standard drink, throughout the rest of this book.

As mentioned earlier, units of alcohol allow a comparison between drinks with different alcohol contents. In the UK it is now common to see labels showing how many units a bottle or serving of a drink holds, such as the one illustrated here.

However, it can still be difficult to know how much alcohol is being consumed with such a range of alcohol contents and glass sizes. For the majority who drink alcoholic beverages, it is a good idea once in a while to check how many units are being consumed. Just think of the new opportunities for small-talk in the pub or when dining out.

"Mine's got 1.6 units, how about yours?"

"Ah, mine's only one unit, but it is Japanese."

No I am not seriously suggesting it as a topic of conversation, but the facts and figures given in the rest of this book on health benefits and risks will mean little if you do not have some idea of what you normally consume. Just check once what your regular drinks contain, so that you know where you stand. When you have read this book, you can judge for yourself what benefits or risks your level of drinking may elicit. In most cases, for moderate consumers, I hope checking units will actually provide peace of mind. For the minority who find they are drinking on the heavy side, hopefully it will be a wake-up call.

To calculate how many units of alcohol are in a drink you need to know the alcoholic content of the beverage and the volume consumed. For example, a bottle of beer might say '4.2% ABV' or a bottle of wine might say '13.5% alc vol'. All bottles show the volume of contents, usually in millilitres, centiliters or litres, such as '330ml' on a bottle of beer, '75cl' on a bottle of wine or '1 Litre' on a bottle of spirits. There are 1000 millilitres (ml) in a litre (l) and 10ml in a centilitre (cl).

It never ceases to amaze me how the drinks industry and legislation use measurements that you never hear of anywhere else. Who uses centilitres? In wine legislation they also use hectolitres (100 litres) and ares for vineyards. No that is not 'acres' spelt incorrectly, as people often think: it is 100 square metres or 0.01 hectares. In pounds, shillings and pence, that means 10 ares equate to about ¼ acre!

Anyway, in practice, how much alcohol you consume will be a factor of the size of your glass. If you have a favourite set of glasses and know roughly how high you fill them, try measuring your normal serving. Using water (you would not want to waste anything better), either pour your normal measure into a measuring cylinder or weigh the glass with and without the water in grams – the difference is the volume in millilitres.

In a bar or restaurant in the UK, a single measure of spirits is usually 25ml, half a pint is 284ml, a pint is 568ml and for wine the glass size will usually be stated. If the alcohol content is not clearly displayed, you can always ask.

Armed with all this information, the number of units per drink is calculated as:

$$Units = volume\ (ml) \times \%\ ABV \div 1000$$

For example, a 175ml glass of 12% ABV wine computes to: $175 \times 12 \div 1000 = 2.1$ units.

Alternatively, you can use the tables at the end of this chapter!

Now that we have done some maths, it is time to look at some graphs and basic letters. The two important letters when analysing alcohol consumption and health are 'U' and 'J'.

Standard Units/Drinks for
BEER AND CIDER

Alcohol Content (ABV%)	Serving Size						
	½ pint						1 pint
	250ml	284ml	300ml	330ml	440ml	500ml	568ml
½	0.1	0.1	0.1	0.2	0.2	0.2	0.3
1	0.2	0.3	0.3	0.3	0.4	0.5	0.6
1½	0.4	0.4	0.4	0.5	0.7	0.7	0.8
2	0.5	0.6	0.6	0.7	0.9	1.0	1.1
2½	0.6	0.7	0.7	0.8	1.1	1.2	1.4
3	0.7	0.8	0.9	1.0	1.3	1.5	1.7
3½	0.9	1.0	1.0	1.1	1.5	1.7	2.0
4	1.0	1.1	1.2	1.3	1.7	2.0	2.2
4½	1.1	1.3	1.3	1.5	2.0	2.2	2.5
5	1.2	1.4	1.5	1.6	2.2	2.5	2.8
5½	1.4	1.5	1.6	1.8	2.4	2.7	3.1
6	1.5	1.7	1.8	2.0	2.6	3.0	3.4
6½	1.6	1.8	1.9	2.1	2.8	3.2	3.6
7	1.7	2.0	2.1	2.3	3.0	3.5	3.9
7½	1.8	2.1	2.2	2.4	3.3	3.7	4.2
8	2.0	2.2	2.4	2.6	3.5	3.9	4.5
8½	2.1	2.4	2.5	2.8	3.7	4.2	4.8
9	2.2	2.5	2.7	2.9	3.9	4.4	5.0
9½	2.3	2.7	2.8	3.1	4.1	4.7	5.3
10	2.5	2.8	3.0	3.3	4.3	4.9	5.6

Standard Units/Drinks for
SPIRITS & FORTIFIED DRINKS[2]

Alcohol Content (ABV%)	Serving size					Bottle 700ml	Bottle 750ml
	25ml	35ml	50ml	75ml	100ml		
17½	0.4	0.6	0.9	1.3	1.7	12.1	12.9
20	0.5	0.7	1.0	1.5	2.0	13.8	14.8
22½	0.6	0.8	1.1	1.7	2.2	15.5	16.6
25	0.6	0.9	1.2	1.8	2.5	17.3	18.5
27½	0.7	0.9	1.4	2.0	2.7	19.0	20.3
30	0.7	1.0	1.5	2.2	3.0	20.7	22.2
32½	0.8	1.1	1.6	2.4	3.2	22.4	24.0
35	0.9	1.2	1.7	2.6	3.5	24.2	25.9
37½	0.9	1.3	1.8	2.8	3.7	25.9	27.7
40	1.0	1.4	2.0	3.0	3.9	27.6	29.6
42½	1.0	1.5	2.1	3.1	4.2	29.3	31.4
45	1.1	1.6	2.2	3.3	4.4	31.1	33.3
47½	1.2	1.6	2.3	3.5	4.7	32.8	35.1
50	1.2	1.7	2.5	3.7	4.9	34.5	37.0

2   A standard bottle of spirits usually contains 700ml. Port and sherry are usually sold in 750ml bottles.

Standard Units/Drinks for
WINE

Alcohol Content (ABV%)	Serving size							
	100ml	125ml	150ml	175ml	200ml	225ml	250ml	Bottle 750ml
8	0.8	1.0	1.2	1.4	1.6	1.8	2.0	5.9
8½	0.8	1.0	1.3	1.5	1.7	1.9	2.1	6.3
9	0.9	1.1	1.3	1.6	1.8	2.0	2.2	6.7
9½	0.9	1.2	1.4	1.6	1.9	2.1	2.3	7.0
10	1.0	1.2	1.5	1.7	2.0	2.2	2.5	7.4
10½	1.0	1.3	1.6	1.8	2.1	2.3	2.6	7.8
11	1.1	1.4	1.6	1.9	2.2	2.4	2.7	8.1
11½	1.1	1.4	1.7	2.0	2.3	2.6	2.8	8.5
12	1.2	1.5	1.8	2.1	2.4	2.7	3.0	8.9
12½	1.2	1.5	1.8	2.2	2.5	2.8	3.1	9.2
13	1.3	1.6	1.9	2.2	2.6	2.9	3.2	9.6
13½	1.3	1.7	2.0	2.3	2.7	3.0	3.3	10.0
14	1.4	1.7	2.1	2.4	2.8	3.1	3.5	10.4
14½	1.4	1.8	2.1	2.5	2.9	3.2	3.6	10.7
15	1.5	1.8	2.2	2.6	3.0	3.3	3.7	11.1
15½	1.5	1.9	2.3	2.7	3.1	3.4	3.8	11.5
16	1.6	2.0	2.4	2.8	3.2	3.6	3.9	11.8

6

Knowing Your Letters – 'U' & 'J'

The results from epidemiological studies are often presented
as graphs. Studies assessing the effects of alcohol on mortality and some specific illnesses frequently exhibit a similar pattern, graphically. This is because a common trend repeatedly
emerges, with light to moderate drinkers showing a lower
risk than either abstainers or heavy drinkers. On a graph this
relationship looks like the one below, and has been termed
the 'U-shaped curve'.

U-shaped curve

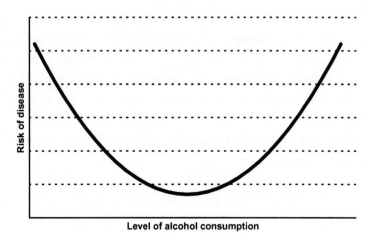

Risk of disease

Level of alcohol consumption

More recently researchers have talked about a 'J-shaped curve', because although abstainers may have a greater risk of death from all-causes or a particular disease than moderate drinkers, heavy drinkers often have a higher risk still. The graph below demonstrates this pattern.

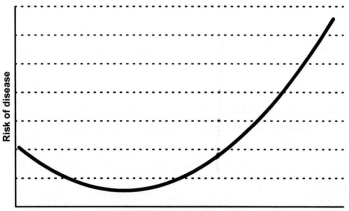

Level of alcohol consumption

This does not apply to epidemiological studies in many other areas. For example, the mortality of smokers rises with increased smoking. Light smokers have higher mortality than non-smokers, moderate smokers have higher mortality than light smokers and heavy smokers have higher mortality still; there is no dip.[1] These U and J-shaped curves are good news; each dip on an epidemiological graph shaped this way represents a range of consumption that is better for you than not drinking alcohol at all. So for drinkers, 'ABV' may stand for 'alcohol by volume' and 'CHD' for 'coronary heart disease',

1   Shavelle R, Paculdo D, Strauss D, Kush S. Smoking habit and mortality: a meta-analysis. Journal of Insurance Medicine. 2008;40:170-8

but 'U' and 'J' stand for 'health'!

There are some other features of these U or J-shaped curves which provide useful information. Up until now, most of the time we have talked about moderate drinkers, or maybe light to moderate drinkers, having a lower risk of dying. But how do we define 'moderate' drinking? In the 1920s, Raymond Pearl was willing to define 'moderate' as up to a bottle of claret a day. In the nineteenth century, many doctors in France were happy for manual workers to drink 2 litres of wine per day. Alas, few modern studies would be quite as generous as that.

Two points on a typical U or J curve are of interest. The first is the nadir. This is the lowest point on the curve, defining the level of drinking that gives the greatest benefit.

The second point of interest is the position on the curve where the risk of death or disease is the same as for an abstainer. I will call this the 'no gain/no loss' point. Many people would see this as an intuitive upper limit for moderate drinking. After all, if the relationship is U or J-shaped, drinking up to the no gain/no loss point will confer some degree of benefit.

Other upper limits for moderate drinking have been suggested. One research paper suggests that the limit for sensible drinking should be 5% above the nadir rather than the no gain/no loss point. Another recommendation from researchers is the point where the rising part of the curve starts to get steep. A steepening curve would suggest that for each additional drink the risk to health is increasing more rapidly. However, accurately establishing that point is difficult.

Of course, one might ask whether there is a right or

wrong definition of moderate drinking. In many areas of
life we have to decide individually whether we will take risks.
How far will you walk to a pedestrian crossing rather than
skipping between the cars? On dietary issues, how closely do
you watch your intake of fat, or salt, or sugar, etc?

I will stick with trying to explain where the nadir and no
gain/no loss points are. I will leave you to decide what level
of risk you want to take.

In the Di Castelnuovo et al meta-analysis of 34 studies,[2]
the authors generated a number of results as they allowed
for the various levels of adjustment in the individual studies
for variables such as age, gender, social status, country of
study, etc. Depending on the precise adjustments carried out,
the nadir across all these different J-shaped curves ranged
from half a standard drink a day to 1¼ standard drinks a day.
Typically the nadir was a little under one standard drink per
day with the figure for women being only a fraction less than
for men.

In a study by White et al in 2002, researchers arrived at
similarly low drinking levels for the nadir.[3] Their research
looked at the change of nadir with age, rising from zero
below age 25 to around half a unit per day for older women
and a little over one unit per day for older men.

Of course, individual studies will have had nadirs higher
and lower than the averaged results. In a 1995 paper, a separate analysis of data from 2 British studies found the nadir
for all-cause mortality in middle-aged men to be 4 units per

2   Di Castelnuovo A, Costanzo S, Bagnardi V, Donati M, Iacoviello L, de Gaetano G.
Alcohol dosing and total mortality in men and women: an updated meta-analysis of 34
prospective studies. Archives of Internal Medicine. 11-25 Dec 2006; 166(22):2437-45.

3   White I, Altmann D, Nanchahal K. Alcohol consumption and mortality: modeling
risks for men and women at different ages. BMJ. 27 Jul 2002; 325:1-7

day.[4] Nevertheless, averages give an indication of where most research results lie.

This may seem surprisingly low, but this is the level of drinking that the research is suggesting for maximum longevity overall. It is worth a reminder at this point that we are still talking about mortality from all causes. We will look at specific diseases and causes of death later.

Estimates of the average no gain/no loss point vary much more. Depending on how and if the results are adjusted in the Di Castelnuovo meta-analysis, the range is between one standard drink and 8½ standard drinks a day. In adjusted studies, for women the no gain/no loss point is between one standard drink and 3½ standard drinks per day. For men the range is between about 3½ and 7 standard drinks per day. Overall, for men and women combined, when ex-drinkers are excluded from the reference group the no gain/no loss average is a little under 4 standard drinks a day. It is difficult to arrive at an exact figure, but taken together these data might suggest a cautious estimate of the no gain/no loss daily drinking level of around 2 standard drinks for women and around 4 standard drinks for men. For women that equates to about a 175ml glass of 12% ABV wine or a pint of 3½% ABV beer per day; for men those quantities would be doubled.

One of the issues about any drinking guideline is that it does not represent a line in the sand. You do not suddenly move from no risk to your health to a significant risk to your health at a particular level of drinking. Guidelines are guidelines.

---

4   Duffy JC. Alcohol consumption and all-cause mortality. International Journal of Epidemiology. Feb 1995; 24(1):100-5.

Cancer in the Curves

Simple-sounding U or J-curves for all-cause mortality provide a straightforward description of the relationship between longevity and alcohol, but they do not give any insight into the balance of various positive and negative consequences of drinking. Not only that, they do not take any account of ill health. We clearly need to consider benefits or harm to quality of life as well as mortality.

It is unlikely to come as a shock to many that heavy drinking is deleterious to health, both in terms of premature death and conditions that seriously decrease the quality of life. Most areas of health that are linked to alcohol show a negative effect for heavy drinkers, although by no means all. For example, a notable exception is coronary heart disease. Most studies in this area show that even for heavy drinkers there remains a benefit, or at least no disadvantage, compared with abstainers.[1]

To understand why the risk of all-cause mortality dips with low to moderate drinking before rising again with heavier drinking, we need to look at the major areas of health that are linked to positive outcomes from drinking, those that

---

1   Marmot M. Alcohol and coronary heart disease. International Journal of Epidemiology. 2001; 30:724-9

are linked to negative outcomes and how the benefits and increased risks interact on overall mortality risk.

THE GOOD

The biggest factor decreasing the risk of dying is the positive effect on cardiovascular disease, in particular coronary heart disease. The reason this association is so important is that more people in developed countries die of cardiovascular disease than anything else, so a large number of deaths are prevented when cardiovascular risk is lowered. World Health Organization data for 2002 puts the cardiovascular deaths figure in the UK at 38%, in the USA at 38% and in Australia at 37% of all deaths.[2] Of these cardiovascular deaths, the greatest killer is coronary heart disease which, as we have already noted, responds positively to alcohol consumption even at heavy drinking levels. It is interesting to consider that a century or two ago, when our diets were very different and coronary heart disease was not the major killer it is today, this benefit of alcohol would have been far less important. Indeed, it remains less significant for developing countries today. The benefits from drinking alcohol many years ago would probably have revolved more around the safety of drinking wine or beer compared with what passed as drinking water. But now, reducing cardiovascular disease is the number one benefit.

Also under the heading of cardiovascular disease are strokes. Ischemic strokes are caused by a blood vessel in the brain becoming blocked which prevents oxygen getting to part of the brain. The other major type of stroke is a haem-

2   World Health Organization – Department of Measurement and Health Information 2004. Table 1: Estimated total deaths by cause and WHO member state 2002.

orrhagic stroke where a blood vessel in the brain ruptures causing bleeding in part of the brain tissue. Light to moderate alcohol consumption has a positive effect on ischemic strokes, which are by far the more common type of stroke. This is another positive outcome from moderate drinking, although the benefit may accrue more to women than to men.[3] However, unlike coronary heart disease, heavy drinking increases the risk of strokes, contributing to the rising part of the U or J-curve at heavier consumption.

Alcohol shows benefits with a number of other diseases, such as the positive effect on type 2 diabetes mellitus,[4] but the reduction in cardiovascular disease is the predominant area where deaths are reduced for moderate drinkers. We should not forget, however, that afflictions such as strokes and diabetes have a huge effect on people's quality of life too. Ischemic strokes often lead to disability. Diabetes can lead to a number of health problems including damaged vision and heart complications.

THE BAD AND THE UGLY

The main areas of chronic disease with links to drinking are some cancers and cirrhosis of the liver. The prime cancer suspects are malignancies of the gastrointestinal tract, such as mouth and throat cancer, together with cancer of the liver. In 1988, the International Agency for Research on Cancer (IARC), which is the cancer research agency of the World Health Organization (WHO), listed the cancers it believed

---

3   Reynolds K, Lewis L, Nolen J, Kinney G, Sathya B, He J. Alcohol consumption and risk of stroke. JAMA. 5 Feb 2003; 289(5):579-88

4   Carlsson S, Hammar N, Grill V. Alcohol consumption and type 2 diabetes. Diabetologia. 2005; 48:1051-54

could be caused by alcohol consumption; they were cancers
of the oral cavity, pharynx, larynx, oesophagus and liver.[5] In
2007, the IARC added breast cancer and colorectal cancer to
this list.[6] Other chronic effects of heavy drinking often stem
from the fact that many alcoholics suffer from malnutrition.
An example is Wernicke's encephalopathy, caused by a lack of
thiamine (vitamin B1), which causes eye movement disorders,
lack of co-ordination, confusion and memory loss.

The acute affects of alcohol are also combined into these
'average' curves, including the devastating loss of life from
drink-related driving accidents. Young people tend to bear
the brunt of the statistics on drink-related driving accidents
and other injuries. There is little doubt that age changes the
distribution of risks and advantages of drinking.

Finally, there are the psychological disorders that are
related to drink, which cause great harm to those with the
conditions and can also devastate their families.

RELATIVE RISKS

Most studies describe the effects of alcohol on a disease as
a relative risk; that is the additional (or decreased) risk that
a drinker has over an abstainer of developing, or dying of,
a particular condition. It is important to understand the
difference between a relative risk and the overall likelihood
of developing a disease. For example, if one in every 100
people dies of a particular disease then an increased relative
risk for drinkers of 50% would mean 1½ in every 100 drink-

5   IARC monographs on the evaluation of carcinogenic risks to humans.
Vol 44(1988) – Alcohol Drinking.

6   IARC Press release 175. 28 Mar 2007. (www.iarc.fr/en/media-centre/pr/2007/
pr175.html)

ers will die of this disease. If the increased relative risk were 300% that would mean 4 in every 100 drinkers will die of the disease. Similarly, if 30 in every 100 people die of a disease then a 20% reduction in the relative risk for drinkers would mean only 24 in every 100 drinkers die of the disease. Relative risks for drinkers only show how likely they are to die of a disease compared to those that do not drink; they do not tell you how many people usually die of that disease.

The increased risks of cancers and liver cirrhosis are the major factors that make the all-cause mortality curves rise with heavier drinking. If we add some numbers, it is easy to see how the curves start to take shape. In 2002, a review article by Rehm et al presented a summary table of the relative risks for a number of chronic diseases known to be affected by alcohol.[7] This table later appeared prominently in the WHO Global Status Report on Alcohol 2004. Health risks were based on three drinking categories. The lowest category was up to 2½ standard drinks per day for a woman and up to 5 standard drinks per day for a man; we will assume this category roughly equates to 'moderate drinking' for the purposes of examining these research results. The next category above 'moderate drinking' went up to 5 standard drinks per day for a woman and 7½ for a man with the highest category being any drinking above these thresholds.

These figures bear out that with coronary heart disease there is limited risk even at high levels of drinking. The benefit in relation to coronary heart disease remains at about a 17% decrease in risk for the lower two categories of drinking

---

7   Rehm J, Room R, Graham K, Monteiro M, Gmel G, Sempos C. The relationship of average volume of alcohol consumption and patterns of drinking to burden of disease: an overview. Addiction. 2003; 98:1209-28

with no loss of benefit for men even in the highest category
and only a 12% added risk for the heaviest-drinking women.

The data on strokes is less forgiving, particularly for
women and haemorrhagic strokes: the more than a third reduction in risk for the lower two categories of female drinker
suddenly gives way to a whopping 700% increased risk for
the heaviest.

When we turn to the recognised negative effects on
chronic disease the increased risks for heavier drinking become more the rule than the exception.

For those in the heaviest drinking category, the risk of
cirrhosis of the liver is 13 times that of non-drinkers – ie
a 1200% increase in risk – whereas moderate drinkers only
have a 30% greater risk. Similarly, mouth and oropharynx
cancers in the heaviest drinkers are up more than 400% as
opposed to 45% in moderate drinkers.

These numbers clearly demonstrate why the U or J
curves start to rise steeply for heavier drinking. With all
the cancers, the risks increase with increased daily alcohol
consumption. And even with some of the positive effects of
alcohol, the heavy drinkers end up paying a price. The cardiovascular benefits of drinking make the all-cause mortality
curves dip for moderate alcohol consumption and the greatly
increased risks from particular cancers and liver cirrhosis
make the curves rise ever steeper for heavier drinking. The
curves represent the combination of the cardiovascular benefits and the increased cancer risks across the spectrum of
drinking levels from abstainer to alcoholic.

But let's not concentrate on the fate of heavy drinkers.
There is little argument that the overall net effects of heavy

drinking are deleterious to health. This sways most of the arguments about alcohol. But that is not what this book is about; I want to look at the case for moderate drinking. So what does this mean for moderate drinkers?

MODERATE DRINKERS

The figures in Table A below, based on the review article mentioned earlier, show the increased risks of the major chronic diseases associated with a negative effect of moderate alcohol consumption (the lowest drinking category in this report): specific cancers, cirrhosis of the liver and hypertension (high blood pressure).

Table A: Increased risks for moderate drinkers compared with abstainers

	Increased risk
Mouth & oropharynx cancers	45%
Oesophageal cancer	80%
Liver cancer	45%
Breast cancer (female only)	14%
Cirrhosis of the liver	30%
Hypertension	40%

The first thing to notice is that when you restrict analysis to moderate drinkers, none of the numbers are that large; neither the increased risks for chronic diseases like cancers nor the reduced risks for the 'good' effects. All the numbers are modest. The greatest risk is for oesophageal cancer at 1.8 times the risk of a non-drinker. In 2002 there were about 8,200 deaths from oesophageal cancer in the UK, about

1.4% of all deaths. Whilst this is not insignificant, it bears no comparison with the number of deaths from cardiovascular diseases – where alcohol generally bestows a benefit on moderate drinkers.

These smaller numbers start to set the whole issue of moderate drinking in some type of perspective. There may well be modest benefits and modestly increased risks, but they are just that – modest. We are no longer looking at the '13 times greater chance of getting liver cirrhosis' that grabs your attention if you look at heavier drinking.

Let us stand back for a moment and think about these numbers, these quite small relative benefits or increased risks. Firstly they are averages. Some studies will have found smaller or non-existent risks or benefits. Certainly some must have found larger risks or benefits, but we must not treat these numbers as set in stone. They are estimates.

Secondly, as already discussed, it is extremely difficult to isolate the effects of alcohol alone. Some of these diseases have been studied for decades – most notably those areas linked to the heart and blood vessels. For this reason, the alcohol-related benefits for heart disease stand as more reliable than much of the data in other areas. Hopefully, with sufficient, varied lines of enquiry there will be better adjustment for confounding factors leading to clearer results. Further research may also provide plausible mechanisms for how alcohol affects all the various conditions.

Thirdly, do not forget that overall, moderate drinkers live longer than non-drinkers, even if alcohol consumption slightly alters the distribution of deaths caused by, say, heart disease as opposed to cancer.

Returning to numbers, when you start to take into account the prevalence of the various diseases that are thought to be affected by alcohol consumption, it is some of the smaller numbers that deserve the most attention. The reason a modest reduction in heart disease is important is because so many people die of it. In the debit column, the 14% increased risk of breast cancer for moderate drinking females is significant. Current figures suggest about one in 10 women in the developed world will get breast cancer during their lifetimes,[8] so even a small increase in risk is worthy of note. Breast cancer is discussed in more detail in a later chapter.

You will notice that no figure was given for the increased risk of colorectal cancer, because at the time of Rehm et al's report (2002) they did not consider that there was sufficient evidence for a causal link between alcohol and colorectal cancer. As mentioned, since then the IARC has added colorectal cancer to their list of cancers that can be caused by drinking alcoholic beverages. The IARC estimates that drinking more than 6 units per day increases the risk of colorectal cancer by about 40%,[9] but this level of drinking is above what most would consider moderate drinking. The IARC also admits that the shape of the graph of colorectal cancer risk versus alcohol consumption is uncertain.

One of the two reports on which the IARC based its

---

8   Collaborative group on hormonal factors in breast cancer. Alcohol, tobacco and breast cancer – collaborative reanalysis of individual data from 53 epidemiological studies, including 58515 women with breast cancer and 95067 women without the disease. British Journal of Cancer. 2002; 87(11):1234-45

9   IARC monographs. Vol 96(2007) – Consumption of alcoholic beverages. Section 5.2.

conclusions,[10] a pooled analysis of 8 cohort studies, states
that the additional risk of colorectal cancer was limited to
those that drank more than about 4 units per day.[11] The other
study, a 2007 meta-analysis, found a similar level of increased
risk when looking at heavier drinkers, but also found some
risk for moderate drinkers.[12] So although colorectal cancer
can be added to the list of woes for heavy drinkers, it is less
certain that there is significant risk for moderate drinkers.

It might also be worth noting that there is a long list of
cancers that the IARC does not have convincing evidence of
their being caused by alcohol. In 2007, this list was: cancers
of the lung, stomach, kidney, pancreas, cervix, endometrium,
ovary, vulva, vagina, male breast, urinary bladder, prostate,
testis, brain and thyroid together with non-Hodgkin's lym-
phoma, skin melanoma, Hodgkin's disease, leukaemias and
multiple myeloma.[13]

Overall, moderate drinkers are better off. The worst-
case scenario is that all the benefits of moderate drinking may
be partly offset by modest increases in the risk of particular
cancers, specifically of the gastrointestinal tract. In the 1995
UK Government report, Sensible Drinking, the team of experts considered that the evidence showed that alcohol does
increase the risk of cancers of the mouth and throat and

10   Baan R, Straif K, Grosse Y, Secretan B, El Ghissassi F, Bouvard V, Altieri A,
Cogliano V, on behalf of the WHO International Agency for Research on Cancer
Monograph Working Group. Carcinogenicity of alcoholic beverages. Lancet Oncology.
Apr 2007; 8(4):292-3

11   Cho E, Smith-Warner S, Ritz J, van den Brandt P, Colditz G et al. Alcohol intake
and colorectal cancer: a pooled analysis of 8 cohort studies. Annals of Internal Medicine. 20 Apr 2004; 140(8):603-13.

12   Moskal A, Norat T, Ferrari P, Riboli E. Alcohol intake and colorectal cancer risk:
a dose-response meta-analysis of published cohort studies. International Journal of
Cancer. 1 Feb 2007; 120(3):664-71.

13   IARC monographs. Vol 96(2007) – Consumption of alcoholic beverages.
Section 5.2

possibly the liver, large intestine and breast. For mouth and throat cancers, where at that time the evidence was already compelling, they concluded that there is convincing evidence of an increased risk where alcohol consumption exceeds 5 standard drinks per day. They concluded that the evidence is "less convincing" for intakes of between 2½ and 5 standard drinks per day and that the data does not allow an estimate of risk below 2½ standard drinks per day although a small increase in relative risk cannot be excluded. Finally, they state that:

"The tumour types causally associated with alcohol are relatively rare in the United Kingdom and thus the number of cases which could be attributed to low levels of drinking would be very small." [14]

You must decide the level of drinking with which you are comfortable, but the evidence indicates that there is a band of low to moderate alcohol consumption that provides cardiovascular benefits, might increase some cancer risks modestly, but overall helps you live longer. If your consumption falls in that moderate drinking band, you are more likely to be doing yourself some good than some harm.

---

14   UK Department of Health. Sensible Drinking: The report of an inter-departmental working group. Dec 1995: pp52-65. Reproduced under the terms of the Click-Use Licence.

8

Bingeing

We are seeing that the amount of alcohol consumed can have beneficial or deleterious effects on health. Emerging from the midst of a sea of statistics, moderate drinking looks both healthy and pleasurable. Keeping your weekly alcohol consumption at a responsible level appears to be a winner. But there is one further aspect that we have to confront if we want to consider ourselves moderate drinkers, free from concerns that we are doing ourselves harm.

Most epidemiological studies to-date have measured alcohol consumption based on average intake. However, some more recent research has started to look at patterns of drinking. Is the impact of having a couple of drinks every day the same as downing 14 drinks on a Friday night? Common sense suggests that it is not. For one thing, two drinks are unlikely to make you drunk; 14 will certainly make most people feel more than a little tipsy. And the research is no more reassuring. Although the volume of research is still limited, it looks to be pointing in one direction – bingeing is bad.

The term 'binge-drinking' is so ubiquitous in the media, yet there is no generally accepted definition of what it is. In the popular press, it is perhaps more defined by its effects than a quantification of the amount of alcohol consumed; noisy, aggressive behaviour, vomiting in the street and clogging up accident and emergency departments at weekends are common portrayals of binge-drinking. Familiar though these descriptions may be, they do not provide a guide to the level of drinking that counts as a binge.

Not surprisingly, there is no particular threshold that, once breached, means you are binge-drinking. Presumably there could be binge-drinking, heavy binge-drinking and very heavy binge-drinking; you might prefer a more descriptive scale such as daft, idiotic and down-right moronic. But for research purposes, binge-drinking has to be defined so that any binge-drinking effects can be attributed to a particular level of alcohol consumption. In America, many researchers are using 5 US drinks in one sitting as the threshold for a binge, although some researchers prefer 8 US drinks. Those levels equate to almost 9 UK standard drinks and 14 UK standard drinks respectively. The UK government recognises binge-drinking as more than double the daily drinking guidelines; that makes the binge threshold 8 standard drinks for men and 6 for women. So although it is not possible to define the exact level of single episode drinking that equates to a binge without looking at each individual study's definitions, these figures provide some idea of the levels involved. For example, 9 UK standard drinks equate to one bottle of 12% ABV wine. In many ways I prefer the more subjective definition of binge-drinking: deliberately drinking to excess, or drinking to get drunk.

The acute effects of binge-drinking or getting drunk are largely common sense; injuries, poisonings and violence all increase with acute intoxication, as do social problems. Drunken behaviour inevitably leads to falls and other physical injuries. Drink fuelled verbal injury often leads to violence: calling a bloke's girlfriend 'pig-face' probably won't be well received, except perhaps by a botanist from down-under who might think you are referring to a rather pretty Australian flower. As regularly reported by the media, and backed up by research, binge-drinking is more prevalent amongst young people and particularly young men. The results are all too obvious every weekend. The problem for people that would like to see themselves as responsible drinkers, however, is that even those who drink modest amounts of alcohol on average can get caught in situations that lead to injuries and violence if they binge-drink. One research paper comments, "At low [average] volumes, risks of injuries, driving while drinking, and even alcohol dependence symptoms are largely limited to those who at least occasionally drink heavy quantities."[1] Binge-drinking can open you up to the acute risks of alcohol even if, on average, your consumption of alcohol is not excessive.

The chronic, cumulative effects of binge-drinking have only quite recently started to be better understood. It seems that in the same way that heavy drinking episodes can have negative social effects, they can also affect disease and mortality. It is becoming clear that many of those marvelous benefits of moderate drinking on coronary heart disease are undone by binge-drinking. In other words, moderate drinking must be moderate on each occasion, not just on average.

---

1   Rehm J, Greenfield T, Rogers J. Average volume of alcohol consumption, patterns of drinking, and all-cause mortality: results from the US National Alcohol Survey. American Journal of Epidemiology. 2001; 153(1):64-71 by permission of Oxford University Press.

Binge-drinking has also been implicated as a risk factor for hypertension and there is speculation that the risk of breast cancer, ischemic stroke and depression may be related to drinking pattern as well.

Studies are showing that periodic binge-drinking increases health risks separately from any risks associated with the average level of drinking. For example, in one study, a reduced risk of coronary heart disease was associated with drinking alcohol for men, but for those that also engaged in periodic heavy drinking sessions (13 UK standard drinks or more), their risk of coronary heart disease was more than double that of non-bingers; for women, the results were less clear.[2] In an Australian study, researchers compared those that spread their drinking across the week with those that concentrated it over a day or two, perhaps weekends. Men who consumed one to 5 units a day on 5 or 6 days per week enjoyed more than a 50% reduction in the risk of heart attack or coronary death. Similarly, women who consumed one to 2½ units on 5 or 6 days per week reduced their risk by about half. However, men who drank 11 or more units and women that imbibed 6 or more units per day, on just one or 2 days in the week, doubled their risk.[3] These roughly similar weekly quantities of alcohol yield very different risks; spread your drinking and your risk halves, concentrate your drinking and the risk doubles. In particular, binge-drinking appears to increase the risk of sudden death from cardiac arrest following

2   Murray R, Connett J, Tyas S, Bond R, Ekuma O, Silversides C, Barnes G. Alcohol volume, drinking pattern, and cardiovascular disease morbidity and mortality: is there a U-shaped function? American Journal of Epidemiology. 2002; 155(3):242-8

3   McElduff P, Dobson A. How much alcohol and how often? Population based case-control study of alcohol consumption and risk of a major coronary event. BMJ. 19 April 1997; 314:1159-64

a binge.

It is worth remembering that research into drinking pattern is far less extensive than that covering average alcohol consumption. Drinking pattern might be related to other chronic diseases. What seems clear already is that binge-drinking not only impacts on the prevalence of injuries but also undoes the cardiovascular benefits of moderate alcohol consumption.

To my mind, that means the definition of moderate drinking must not only cover average drinking but the pattern of drinking as well. As far as I can see, if you want to claim you are drinking in moderation you cannot also binge-drink. Logically, frequent binge-drinking, and presumably 'heavier' binge-drinking, is likely to be of greater risk than the occasional slight overindulgence. Nevertheless, for the remainder of this book, I assume that moderate drinking means not only moderate average consumption of alcohol but also avoiding heavier drinking episodes.

But this is not all doom and gloom. For example, if more extensive research shows that hypertension is related largely to binge-drinking, that would mean that for true moderate drinkers, the risks in relation to hypertension would decrease. If breast cancer were found to be related more to heavy drinking episodes than the average level of alcohol consumption, that would be a great finding for true moderate drinkers. Only time will tell, but this type of explanation might shed light on some of the statistics that are already well-known. For example, it might clarify why in those cultures where drinking is daily with meals, such as in France, they have fewer cardiovascular problems than where drinking is more concentrated. Researchers have postulated that this could be a beer versus wine issue, but perhaps it is also to do with drinking pattern – spreading drinking throughout the week versus cramming it in at the weekend.

For cardiovascular disease, where the effects of drinking pattern are already a little better understood, the results are again good news for true moderate drinkers. If the risk curves are showing net benefits for those who on average drink moderately, that implies that if you separate out the binge-drinkers with moderate average consumption the true moderate drinkers will have an even greater benefit from their drinking.

The pattern of drinking may also go some way to explaining the range of cardiovascular protection levels that different studies have found. It is possible that some study populations have a higher proportion of binge-drinkers than others, which could decrease the reported protection effect for true moderate drinkers.

I realise I may have dashed the hopes of a number of the Friday-night drinkers; those that 'only' get drunk once a week. On the other hand, I cannot believe that too many of you were really deluding yourselves into thinking that getting sozzled at the weekend but being teetotal for the rest of the week is a healthy and balanced way to carry on. If you did, I am sorry; but the long-and-short of it is that bingeing is bad. If I were asked to speculate, I would suggest that as more research is undertaken on drinking patterns, the absence of binge-drinking will become an increasingly important aspect of defining low-risk drinking.

9

Improving Your Odds?

Chapter 7 provided some statistics on the increased risks for
various diseases that are linked to alcohol consumption and
drive the rising section of U or J-shaped all-cause mortality
curves. This chapter looks a little further at alcohol-related
deaths and injuries from accidents and deliberate violence,
together with alcoholism. These causes of death also contribute to the shape of the curves.

There are two reasons for examining these issues. Firstly,
they are widely associated with alcohol misuse and, in the
case of accidents and violence, account for a significant proportion of alcohol-related deaths. Secondly, although these
issues are extremely serious, they are unlikely to impact all
drinkers equally. As with the rest of this book, the intended
focus here is on moderate drinkers. How should the risks of
injury and alcoholism affect moderate drinkers' attitudes to
how much they consume?

INJURIES

Accidents account for around a quarter of all alcohol-related
deaths.[1] At younger ages, injuries account for a much larger

---

1   UK Department of Health. Sensible Drinking: The report of an inter-departmental
working group. Dec 1995: p17

proportion of alcohol-related deaths than at older ages. For men/boys aged 16 to 24, in England and Wales, injuries account for a staggering 97% of all alcohol-attributable deaths.[2] Of course, to put that in some perspective, regardless of alcohol intake, accidents and violence are the biggest cause of death in young people. In a Swedish survey of mostly 18 and 19 year old male conscripts, 75% of all deaths in the following 15 years were violent deaths – caused by accidents, suicide, drownings, murders, etc.[3] Chronic diseases have not caught up with young people this early in their lives so injuries are the major causes of premature death.

These tragic deaths and the many non-lethal injuries cannot be ignored, but they are not an obvious consequence of moderate drinking. They represent acute effects of drinking alcohol and are linked to how much is consumed on a single occasion and the social context for that drinking. Clearly injuries are more likely if you are staggering around drunk, verbally abusing everyone within earshot – falls and fights are bound to follow. As was discussed in the previous chapter, binge-drinking is strongly associated with injuries regardless of average drinking levels.

You only need to watch one of the many television programmes about young people and drinking to see that the way some are consuming alcohol, accidents are inevitable. You see young people on pub-crawls, gulping spirits like they are drinking mild ale and undergoing 'challenges' like downing a pint of urine – and not even their own. For some, the

2   White I, Altmann D, Nanchahal K. 'Optimal' levels of alcohol consumption for men and women at different ages, and the all-cause mortality attributable to drinking. Alcohol Education & Research Council (www.aerc.org.uk). 2002

3   Andreasson S, Allebeck P, Romelsjo A. Alcohol and mortality among young men: longitudinal study of Swedish conscripts. BMJ. 9 Apr 1988; 296:1021-5

whole intention of drinking is to get drunk, with fighting all part of a night out and the hospital's accident and emergency department a familiar end to the activities.

The quantities of alcohol that are being drunk, tens of units in an evening, are staggering. Earlier in this book I mentioned that ethanol poisoning is quite hard to achieve; you have to drink a lot over a relatively short time period without being sick. Yet people do die of alcohol poisoning. Certainly some of these youths are taking big risks. They should not be worrying about cirrhosis of the liver or possible increases in cancer: they should worry about lasting out the night.

Accidents and violence are the acute, or immediate, effects of drinking alcohol. They are less about how much you drink on average; they are about how much you drink in one session and where that drinking takes place. It is obvious to all that injuries are more likely after a period of heavy drinking, but we have already ascertained that binge-drinking is a likely cause of wide-ranging health risks and not something that can be considered part of 'moderate' drinking.

For the moderate drinker, that leaves the drinking context as a risk factor for accidents and violence. For example, alcohol will have an effect on driving, using machinery or swimming; moderate drinking needs to be accompanied by common sense. Take swimming as an example. Drownings after drinking are quite common. Yet if you know you have had a few drinks, you can simply avoid swimming and therefore avoid drowning. Attitude and the company kept are all very important when looking at the acute affects of alcohol consumption. Even if you do drink too much in responsible company, they will see that you do not come to grief – although they will probably keep the photographs to pass round at the next social event you attend! Go out with a pack of wild animals and you are in for trouble even if you drink orange juice all night.

Of course, we are all exposed to risk from those that behave badly under the influence of alcohol, whether walking through a town centre or driving home. But someone else's behavior is not going to be modified by your level of drinking. Unless you get so agitated by people drinking irresponsibly that you drink yourself into oblivion, your drinking level is not going to affect the risk they pose to you one iota.

To minimise the risk of injuries, drinking should be moderate on each occasion as well as on average; in other words, as already discussed, do not binge. For all moderate drinkers, care should be taken to avoid situations that are potentially risky – but that is just common sense. For young drinkers, the statistics are not in their favour. Nevertheless, the guidelines really do not differ much from those for older drinkers, although peer pressure may make it more difficult to put them into practice.

Due to the high level of alcohol-related injuries for younger people, the benefits of drinking alcohol are skewed towards older folk. However, if young people can avoid many of the injury risks, moderate alcohol consumption in itself is not a problem. The Swedish study of young men mentioned earlier showed a strong correlation between alcohol consumption and mortality. Yet when the 75% of violent deaths are stripped out, the study recognises that the data "suggested" a U-shaped curve. Even for the young, if accidents and injuries can be avoided, moderate drinking does not do any harm.

ALCOHOLISM

Alcoholism is another serious affliction that some drinkers develop. One of the main arguments against promoting the benefits of moderate drinking is that some moderate drinkers may turn into alcoholics. But there are plenty of moderate drinkers that are quite stable in their drinking habits. If we stopped everything, just because we might overdo it, life would be rather limiting: no chocolate – you might overdo it and get fat; no painkillers – you might overdose; no salt, you might overdo it and get hypertension. It may seem strange, but people have even died from drinking too much water; the brain can swell up in a condition called cerebral oedema.

Any definition of moderate drinking must exclude a level of drinking that equates to being an alcoholic. Therefore, if a moderate drinker moves towards alcohol dependency, at some point that person must begin drinking more. When that starts, the drinker can make the decision to revert to drinking less. Even if it happens without the 'moderate' drinker really noticing, once he or she realises, or is told, things are getting out of hand, he or she can cut back. That is not to suggest it is easy, but plenty of people do reduce or quit drinking, smoking, gambling, etc. The point is that there is a behavioral element that means that even if the statistics show an increased risk of alcoholism for moderate drinkers, it does not have to apply to you. As already mentioned, it is a good idea every now and then to check you know how much you are drinking. If you are armed with that information, how much you decide to drink is within your control.

Another example of a behaviour that can get out of hand is spending on credit cards. Credit cards are a convenient way to make purchases. But if you lose control, and many people do, you can end up spending more than you can pay off, potentially leading to terrible, debilitating indebtedness. I do not have any figures to quote, but surely there must be an increased statistical risk of getting into problem debt if you use credit cards; the temptation of easy credit is always there. But do you worry about sensible, 'moderate' if you will, credit card spending? If you have a little self-control and don't 'max out' your plastic, why worry about spending on credit cards?

Surely the same applies to drinking. Sensible, moderate drinking can lead to heavier drinking and alcoholism, but if you have some self-control it does not need to.

AVOIDING INJURIES AND ALCOHOLISM

For moderate drinkers that apply some common sense, the chance of avoiding alcohol-related accidents or violence is likely to be better than average. Similarly, if you keep in control of your drinking and check periodically that you are not overdoing it, is it really worth worrying about your risk of becoming an alcoholic? But what difference does it make whether these increased risks from drinking can be largely avoided or that the burden of alcohol-related injuries lies disproportionately on young people?

The answer is that the average U or J-shaped curves may need modifying for specific groups of people and for you individually. When we looked at the J-curve for all-cause

mortality, we noted that women are generally more sensitive to alcohol than men so their J-curves shows a dip at a
lower alcohol intake than for men. But these curves vary by
age too. At younger ages, deaths from injuries are the most
important factor whereas deaths from heart disease are quite
rare. As a consequence there may hardly be a J-curve for
younger drinkers.

For the majority of moderate drinkers, the risks of most
concern are the chronic diseases, particularly cancers and
hypertension. If alcohol increases these risks slightly, as the
statistics seem to show, there is probably little that we can do
to avoid them for a particular level of drinking. However, if
there are risks that depend, at least partly, on our behaviour,
we can have some impact on our personal risk compared
with the population as a whole; we can tweak our J-curve; we
can improve our odds. If our risks of alcoholism and injury
are small, our net benefit from moderate drinking improves a
little. As we are regularly reminded, every little helps.

10

The Numbers are Wrong!

Whilst studying the data on alcohol, a number of strange statistics stood out. Perhaps the most contradictory was from the World Health Organization (WHO) in its Global Status Report on Alcohol 2004. It shows a table of per capita alcohol consumption for over 180 countries. As you would expect, some Muslim countries show consumption per capita of zero. Amongst those nil-consumers is Iran. Later in the same report is a list of alcohol dependency by country. It came as quite a surprise that Iran was listed as one of the worst countries for alcohol dependence, with a substantial 7.3% of the population addicted to the strong stuff. How do you make sense of that?

Oddities like this will always occur when trying to compare data from different sources. Even your staid statisticians must find a moment of mirth in some of these comparisons.

But I am not talking about occasional irregularities when making the statement that the numbers used in alcohol research are wrong. They are probably all wrong.

The fact is that the figures used in epidemiological studies under-estimate how much people drink. There is little alternative when conducting studies than to ask people how much they consume. There are various ways of extracting the information but they all require respondents to recall their alcohol intake over a period of time or to record it, going forwards, in a diary. Unfortunately, the data tends to be pretty unreliable. The WHO estimates that self-reporting of alcohol consumption understates alcohol consumption by 40% to 60%.[1] It is possible that some heavier drinkers are missed by these surveys, but that is unlikely to account for such a huge disparity. These figures show that, when asked, most people only own up to about half of what they drink.

How can we be sure? We can get accurate figures for the total alcohol consumed in a country from supply side figures. Industry bodies and tax authorities gather information on total sales which can then be divided by the adult population to arrive at the average sales per individual; this figure can then be compared with what people say they drink. Unless there are people that bathe in champagne, use vodka as disinfectant or water their gardens with beer, the figures should be the same.

For example, for 2005/2006 in the UK, Her Majesty's Revenue and Customs estimates that on average, each person over the age of 16 consumed 1140 standard drinks per year.[2] Believe me, they know; they collect revenue off every drop of alcohol that is released for consumption. On top of that, estimates add another 200 standard drinks per year from cross-border shopping, illegal imports and homebrew.[3] That brings the total to 1340 standard drinks per year. However, the General Household Survey 2005, a continuous survey

1   World Health Organization. Global Status Report on Alcohol 2004: p4

2   Statistics on Alcohol: England 2007. The Information Centre (UK National Health Service) p90

3   World Health Organization. Global Status Report on Alcohol 2004: p16

carried out by the Office for National Statistics (ONS), puts the figure at just 563 standard drinks per year (10.8 per week).[4] That means individuals have only reported 42% of what they drink, unless we adhere to the phantom champagne-bather theory.

A portion of the difference is easily explained. Alcohol levels in drinks have increased over the years and the ONS did not keep up, although they have made some adjustments recently. For wine in particular, glass sizes have increased as well. Those 2005 figures still assume one unit of alcohol per glass of wine; that corresponds to a 125ml glass containing wine with an alcoholic strength of 8% ABV. Maybe civil servants, whilst consuming their lunch-time claret at 12% or 13% ABV, still thought the masses drank large quantities of Hock or Asti. In 2007 the ONS updated how it calculates alcohol consumption from survey data. Applying the new method to the 2005 figures would yield an annual consumption of 746 standard drinks (14.3 per week) rather than 563.[5] Nevertheless, this still equates to only 56% of the true figure.

Either way, these figures tend to bear out the view of the WHO, that people underestimate their drinking by around half. Of course, academics have tried various methods to extract more reliable consumption data from the people they are studying. But in most cases, it still falls back on some form of questionnaire or diary. No doubt some will get more accurate results than others, but the clear tendency is for people to under-report.

---

4 Office for National Statistics (UK). General Household Survey 2005. Smoking and drinking among adults, 2005. Nov 2006 p77

5 Office for National Statistics (UK). National Statistics Methodological Series No 37. Estimating alcohol consumption from survey data: updated method of converting volumes to units. Dec 2007. p1

If you are surprised at the lack of recall when reporting alcohol consumption, it is no better when remembering
paying for drinks. The ONS's Family Spending report for
2006 shows that families in the UK reported spending about
£20 billion on alcoholic drinks during the year,[6] whereas data
based on sales puts the figure nearer £42 billion.[7] Again,
individuals seem to only report about 50% of the alcoholic
beverages they purchase.

So what effect does this have on the huge amount of
alcohol-related research? One could argue that if everyone
under-reports their alcohol consumption and thinks they are
drinking less than they really are, then any error in studies
only mirrors what people are actually doing. If a study gives
a finding for alcohol consumption at 2 drinks per day, in reality that finding might apply to 3 or 4 drinks a day (accurately
measured) because the individuals reported as drinking 2
drinks a day, were probably actually drinking 3 or 4 drinks
a day. Furthermore, those people in the wider society that
are drinking 3 or 4 drinks a day, probably think they are only
drinking 2 drinks a day.

But that is all in the averages. In practice there are a
couple of implications. The first is that for those who do
accurately assess how much they are drinking, they need to
reduce that intake figure, perhaps by around half, to compare
their drinking with the academic studies. As government
guidelines are loosely based on the academic research, these
'accurate' drinkers could use the reduced figure in compari-

6   Office for National Statistics (UK). Family Spending: 2006 edition. 1 May 2007.
p61 (data extrapolated)

7   Statistics on Alcohol: England 2007. The Information Centre (UK National Health
Service) pp 79, 80, 91

sons with drinking guidelines too. Put the other way round, even if following government guidelines, you can probably drink quite a lot more than the stated limit, perhaps as much as double, if you know how much you are drinking.

This is another reason why I recommend that, periodically, people accurately assess how much they are drinking. Only when you have a realistic estimate of your alcohol consumption can you decide where you want to place your limit.

The second implication is more difficult to quantify. However, it would seem logical that heavier drinkers are more likely to under-report than lighter drinkers. It stands to reason that heavier drinkers may feel more embarrassed about how much they are drinking or may find it more difficult to recall how much they have drunk. At the extremes of the scale, it is clear that a teetotaller cannot under-report and probable that someone who passes out through alcohol consumption cannot remember how much they drank!

The consequence could be that heavier drinkers get classified as moderate drinkers, therefore causing researchers to overstate the risks to moderate drinkers. Not that much research seems to have been done on this hypothesis. Although this needs testing, it is surely quite likely that those that drink more, are more likely to under-report. We know that collectively this is happening, people are under-reporting; we just need more evidence of the distribution.

So in general, we see that asking people about their alcohol consumption usually elicits an under-estimate of the true figure. This under-estimate can be as low as 40% of the real figure. If you are one of the under-estimators, then the research probably applies to you as published.

However, if you take the time to accurately assess your alcohol intake, you probably have a little more leeway in how much you can drink when looking at research findings or government guidelines.

Regardless of whether you pour with liberality or drink strictly by the measure, there is still an overarching impact on how you should interpret research findings. It is a reasonable assumption that heavier drinkers are more likely to under-report than lighter drinkers. If that is indeed the case, then the risks that are reported for moderate drinkers might just be a little exaggerated.

11

An Unproven Hypothesis

We have seen that widespread under-reporting of alcohol consumption, probably most prevalent in heavy drinkers, may cause studies to overstate risks for moderate drinkers. In addition, if alcohol-related injury is at least partly avoidable and if alcohol dependency is not an automatic consequence of moderate drinking, where does that leave the health risk question for moderate drinkers?

There are still those modest increases to cancer risks. We have already seen that overall, moderate drinkers live longer, largely because of the benefits to the heart and circulation. But even if increased cancer risks are not large and are out-weighed by cardiovascular benefits, no-one wants to see their risk of cancer increase materially.

Well maybe, just maybe, the cancer risks are not greater. I say maybe, because this is an unproven hypothesis, but bear with me for a moment. Many graphs of specific cancer risks look similar to the one in Fig 1. There is an escalating risk of the particular cancer as alcohol consumption increases. The final level of risk at higher drinking levels will vary by cancer and the steepness of the curve will be modified by cancer type and possibly gender. Nevertheless, the shape is typical.

Fig 1. Typical cancer dose-response curve

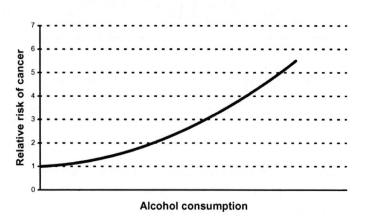

Alcohol consumption

One thing that is immediately clear from these graphs is that there is an increased risk from the first drop of alcohol consumed. You consume one teaspoonful of beer and you have increased your risk of cancer, only a little, but nevertheless your risk has gone up. Swallow a second teaspoonful and you have more than doubled your additional risk of cancer. And so it goes on; with every mouthful of golden nectar, every sip of blood-red wine, every taste of your favourite tipple, you are more likely to get cancer.

Does that ring true to you? Is it not possible that there is a level of alcohol consumption that has no significant adverse effects on your likelihood of getting cancer? There are those that have raised questions about the shape of these cancer risk curves. The team of experts that prepared the Sensible Drinking report for the UK Government in 1995 expressed its views about the lack of convincing data to substantiate increased risks at lower levels of drinking, whilst accepting the risks for heavier drinkers.[1] In a recent paper by Klatsky and Udaltsova, they note that one of the likely effects of under-reporting is to create an apparent continuous relationship in place of a true threshold relationship between alcohol and risk factors.[2]

This is an area of some controversy amongst the alcohol researchers. I understand that there is an analogy used in some research fields that goes something like this. If I drop a cricket ball on your head it will hurt. If I drop a ping-pong ball on your head, it won't hurt less; it won't hurt at all. Heavy drinking will hurt you, but will a light or moderate dose hurt you less? Perhaps it won't hurt at all.

My unproven hypothesis is that there may be no materially adverse effect on cancer risk for those drinking at the lower end of the alcohol consumption spectrum. How can I make such a bold statement? Well, firstly, I am not saying what the risk-free threshold level would be – that would need a lot of work from researchers. But let us go back to those cancer-risk graphs that show an increased risk of cancer from the first tiny drop of alcohol that passes your lips. That seems implausible to me. I realise there are some toxic substances that build up in the body over time; as a consequence, even the tiniest quantity of these substances could be considered to start you on the increased risk path. But alcohol does not build up in the body; it is broken down and then flushed down the toilet. So I find it hard to believe that there is any additional risk when you imbibe your first 5ml of

1   UK Department of Health. Sensible Drinking: The report of an inter-departmental working group. Dec 1995: pp53-4, 64

2   Klatsky A, Udaltsova N. Alcohol drinking and total mortality risk. Annals of Epidemiology. 2007; 17:S63-7

beer. Accepting that there is an increased risk of cancer at
high levels of alcohol consumption, there must be a point at
which risk moves from zero and starts to increase. Presumably this might happen when the body's normal means of
eliminating alcohol starts to be stretched in some way. Ad-
mittedly, it is possible that the level of alcohol consumption
that moves your additional risk above zero may be very small,
in which case those cancer-risk graphs are near enough correct. But is that really why those graphs take on that shape?

At the risk of boring all the non-mathematically minded,
the way researchers arrive at these dose-response graphs, as
they are known, is important. The aim is to find an equation,
a line or curve, that best describes the data. Many different
types of curve may be tried; the simplest would be a straight
line, then perhaps a quadratic or higher order polynomial.
Yet all these curves have one thing in common: they can be
described by a single equation.[3]

Now take a look at Fig 2 below.

Fig 2. Hypothetical cancer dose-response curve

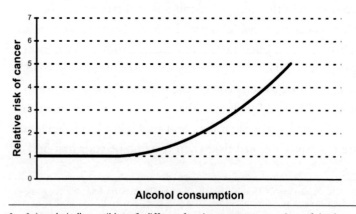

3   It is technically possible to fit different functions to separate portions of the data,
but the usual approach with this type of data is to fit a single function to all the data.

This is a graphical expression of my unproven hypothesis. The left third of the graph is a straight line representing light and moderate drinking with no extra risk. The right two-thirds is an escalating risk curve that represents increased risk for heavier drinking; it has been described by a quadratic equation. The critical point is that this curve is described by a combination of two equations; the straight-line and the quadratic curve. Why is this important? It is important because none of the equations typically used by researchers is capable of generating a curve of that shape. So even if my curve represents the accurate quantification of alcohol-related risk, studies would be unlikely to arrive at that result! To complicate the matter further, the shape of the curve would also be affected by the under-reporting that is so common when collecting data on alcohol consumption.

So what might they conclude if my curve represented the truth? To try to demonstrate what might happen I have added some variation to the underlying data and some under-reporting. In practice there are always random variations and random errors in research data so, using computer-generated random numbers, I added some random variation to my hypothetical dose-response curve.[4] The results are shown in Fig 3 overleaf.

---

4   The initial hypothetical curve was described by 1000 points, distributed evenly along the x-axis (alcohol consumption). To add random variation, the data points were assumed drawn from a normal distribution with mean given by the function in Fig. 2 and standard deviation assumed equal to 15% of the mean risk of cancer.

Fig 3. Hypothetical data with randomisation

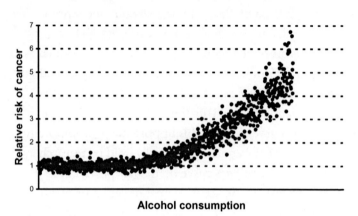

Alcohol consumption

I then added some random under-reporting. You will remember from the previous chapter that the World Health Organization estimates that people generally under-report by between 40% and 60%, and the figures for the UK seem to bear that out. To stay on the cautious side, I assumed that 50% of individuals under-report and these under-reporters actually report between 40% and 80% of their true consumption. These assumptions were again added in random fashion across all the data. In effect, this adjustment only assumes under-reporting of a modest 20% [5] and was applied across all drinking levels. A bigger effect would have been obtained by assuming the under-reporting was more prevalent in heavier drinkers, but to err on the cautious side all drinkers were assumed to be equally likely to under-report their alcohol consumption. The resulting data plots are shown in Fig 4.

5   Under-reporting = 50% x average$\{(1 - 40\%), (1 - 80\%)\} = 20\%$

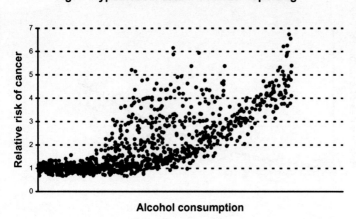

Fig 4. Hypothetical data with under-reporting

Alcohol consumption

The remaining task is to add a curve to fit this data. There are a number of different possible equations that researchers might use, and they would probably also look at closeness of fit.[6] I have kept things simple and used a quadratic curve, which is common in this type of analysis. I have also assumed that at zero alcohol consumption the relative risk must be one, in other words, risk is measured relative to abstainers. The result is shown in Fig 5 overleaf.

As you can see, it looks very like the typical alcohol-related cancer risk curves. Yet this was based on data that showed no risk whatsoever for low and moderate alcohol consumption. This is only an illustration and proves nothing in itself. It does, however, show how with some simple and conservative assumptions applied to data that shows no risk at low and moderate levels of alcohol consumption, it is easy to end up with a graph that indicates an increased risk from the first drop of alcohol consumed.

---

6   Data is also sometimes transformed using logarithms. To maintain clarity and simplicity, this hypothetical data was not transformed.

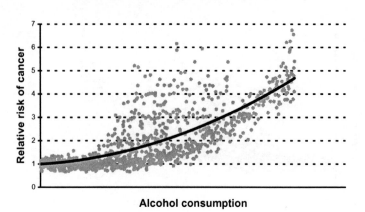

Fig 5. Hypothetical data with curve fitted

Without doubt there are many researchers out there
that could make a much more robust job of looking at this
hypothesis. What surprised me was the ease with which data
showing no risk could result in graphs that show increasing
risk at all levels. I expect there will be experts in this field
that would have something to say on this. Rather than direct
any comments at me, I hope they will just go out and prove,
one way or the other, whether there really is an increased risk
of cancer at low and moderate levels of alcohol consumption. I am sure I am not the only one that would like a convincing answer to this question.

12

Cardiovascular Benefits

The effects of alcohol consumption on cardiovascular disease have probably been studied more than any other impact of alcohol on wellbeing. As previously indicated, this is the area of health where researchers have shown some of the clearest benefits for drinkers. Copious research has been undertaken. The general conclusion from these studies is that consuming alcohol can reduce your risk of cardiovascular disease by as much as 40%.

This is of immense importance in developed countries, where cardiovascular disease is the biggest killer. World Health Organisation statistics for 2002 indicate that cardiovascular disease accounts for about 38% of deaths in the UK, 38% in the USA, 34% in Canada, 37% in Australia, 40% in New Zealand, 48% in Germany, 31% in France and 32% in Japan. In the largest developing countries the position is not much better; the figures are 33% for China and 27% for India. Some of the individual developed country figures for more recent years may have improved slightly, but nevertheless, about a third of all deaths are attributable to cardiovascular disease, ahead of any other cause.

Although epidemiological studies cannot prove a causal relationship absolutely, the volume and variety of studies looking at the link between alcohol and cardiovascular disease benefits is impressive. Of course, cardiovascular disease covers a range of medical conditions that respond to alcohol in different ways and to varying extents. These include:

- Heart attack (myocardial infarction) – the end result of coronary heart disease

- Atherosclerosis – a hardening and narrowing of the arteries caused by fatty deposits in the arterial wall

- Abnormal heart rhythm (arrhythmia)

- Heart muscle disease (cardiomyopathy), sometimes leading to heart failure

- Strokes, both from blocked blood vessels (ischemic stroke) and bleeding (hemorrhagic stroke)

- High blood pressure (hypertension)

- Angina – although this is rarely analysed in these studies because symptoms vary so much

Where alcohol affects health at all, most of the responses to moderate alcohol consumption are positive; there is little evidence of negative effects for moderate drinkers. Interestingly, although there is no doubt that heavy drinking is damaging to health, when it comes to some types of cardiovascular disease, in particular heart attacks, even heavy drinking seems to give positive results. In a meta-analysis published in 2000, researchers found a beneficial effect on heart disease up to 9 units a day;[1] that is about a bottle of wine a day. This is not in anyway to encourage heavy drinking as the other risks, for example liver disease and cancers, must be taken into account. Nevertheless, as far as your heart is concerned, it seems you can drink to your heart's content. Proof is in the dissecting; autopsies on alcoholics often show relatively clean coronary arteries. Some would argue that there is more compelling evidence that moderate to heavy drinking is good for your heart than the more generally accepted light to moderate drinking. Notably, heavier drinking appears to be more beneficial for those at greater risk of cardiovascular disease.[2] There is a logic in this: if the most likely ailment to finish you off is heart disease then you will benefit from anything that tempers that risk. The positive effects of alcohol on heart disease are likely to be more critical than any negative effects in other areas of health, for example, an increased propensity to some cancers.

Apart from the sheer number of epidemiological studies conducted in this area showing health benefits, the other compelling factor is that there are several plausible mechanisms by which alcohol can work its magic. Additional studies, both in humans and in test-tubes, have added to the body of knowledge on how alcohol can provide beneficial cardiovascular disease outcomes. Many of these mechanisms are extremely complicated and scientists are still trying to un-

1   Corrao G, Rubbiati L, Bagnardi V, Zambon A, Poikolainen K. Alcohol and coronary heart disease: a meta-analysis. Addiction. Oct 2000; 95(10):1505-23

2   Thun M, Peto R, Lopez A, Monaco J, Henley S, Heath C, Doll R. Alcohol consumption and mortality among middle-aged and elderly US Adults. The New England Journal of Medicine. 11 Dec 1997; 337(24):1705-14

ravel all the biological processes. What follows is a very brief summary of the major mechanisms that have been explored.

Alcohol is believed to increase the level of HDL (high density lipoproteins or 'good cholesterol') in the blood, which helps to remove fatty deposits from the walls of blood vessels. The process by which this occurs is not fully understood but the resulting increase in HDL has been observed in many studies. Higher HDL levels are clearly beneficial in relation to atherosclerosis.

Alcohol is also thought to protect against the formation of blood clots through lower levels of fibrinogen and an anti-coagulant effect on blood platelets. This has a similar effect to taking aspirin, whereby blood clots more slowly in response to a damaged blood vessel. Alcohol may also have a relaxing effect on the walls of blood vessels, dilating constricted arteries.

These effects of alcohol are thought to provide the majority of the benefits from drinking alcohol for cardiovascular disease. They are associated with any form of alcohol-containing beverage. A further area where researchers believe alcoholic beverages may decrease the risks of cardiovascular disease is through the antioxidants (mainly polyphenols) found particularly in red wine, but also to a lesser extent in white wine, some beers and cider. It is believed that these antioxidants may prevent some of the oxidation of LDL (low density lipoproteins or 'bad cholesterol'), which is part of the metabolic process by which plaque is deposited in artery walls.

All the above mechanisms are beneficial to the reduction in coronary heart disease and, with heart attacks being such a significant cause of death, this has major positive health outcomes.

Heart muscle disease and irregular heart rhythm[3] are not likely to be benefited to any great extent from the mechanisms described above. However, it is thought that any negative effects of alcohol in these areas tend to relate to heavy and binge drinking, not the moderate consumption of alcoholic beverages.

Ischemic stroke is less likely due to the lowering of the build up of arterial plaque and the blood thinning benefits. In women, the reduction in ischemic strokes could be as high as 50%, but for men the benefit is more marginal.[4,5] A reduction in this area is important not just because of the reduced deaths, but also because ischemic strokes are a major cause of ill health and disability. On the other hand, the blood-thinning effects of alcohol may make hemorrhagic strokes more likely, at least in men.

High blood pressure is clearly linked to heavy drinking. Moderate drinking may increase blood pressure although there is some controversy here.[6] Some studies show an increase, some point to an increased risk above a threshold of 4 to 5 standard drinks per day and other studies suggest a J-shaped association between alcohol consumption and blood pressure. Although a wide range of possible mechanisms for

3   Mukamal K, Tolstrup J, Friberg J, Jensen G, Gronbaek M. Alcohol consumption and risk of atrial fibrillation in men and women. Circulation. 20 Sep 2005; 112(12):1736-42

4   Rehm J, Room R, Graham K, Monteiro M, Gmel G, Sempos C. The relationship of average volume of alcohol consumption and patterns of drinking to burden of disease: an overview. Addiction. 2003; 98:1209-28

5   Reynolds K, Lewis L, Nolen J, Kinney G, Sathya B, He J. Alcohol consumption and risk of stroke, a meta-analysis. JAMA. 5 Feb 2003;289(5):579-88

6   Tomson J, Gregory Y. Alcohol and hypertension: an old relationship revisited. Alcohol & Alcoholism. 2006;41(1):3-4

the relationship between drinking and high blood pressure has been put forward, it remains unclear how the association works.

As already mentioned, it is thought that the majority of the benefit of drinking, as it relates to cardiovascular disease, is linked to alcohol rather than a particular beverage. However, the view is growing that regular drinking may be important and that irregular drinking, and in particular binge drinking, may decrease the benefits significantly or even cause net harm.

This is all very positive, but a number of questions may be running through your mind. Do these benefits accrue for all moderate drinkers? What about those that already have heart disease or high blood pressure?

Before making some general comments about categories of drinkers, it is important to state that anyone with an existing medical condition would be well advised to talk through the issue of alcohol consumption with their doctor before coming to any decisions. This is essential if medicines are being taken, as there may be adverse or unexpected outcomes when these are combined with alcohol.

With these provisos in mind, it is interesting to look at what the researchers have to say about different categories of drinkers. For example, alcohol is known to be a contributor to high blood pressure, at least with heavier drinking. Yet for men with high blood pressure that keep their drinking in moderation, they still appear to benefit from lower cardiovascular disease and all-cause mortality than they would do if they gave up alcohol.[7] Increased blood pressure, whether precipitated by alcohol or a number of other causes, would be expected to increase cardiovascular diseases. However, once an individual has high blood pressure, the benefits of continuing to drink in moderation are still evident.

Similarly, people with type 2 diabetes still appear to be able to lower cardiovascular risk through moderate drinking, as do those that already have cardiovascular disease including having suffered a heart attack.[8,9] Indeed, this is a common thread through many studies; those at high risk or already suffering from cardiovascular disease seem to benefit the most from alcohol. Far from giving up alcohol once diagnosed with heart disease, it appears that this is the time to keep drinking, at sensible levels.

Despite all the positive studies showing the cardiovascular benefits of moderate drinking, many still resist any notion that people might be encouraged to drink alcoholic beverages. Usually they are concerned that some of those persuaded to drink may start drinking excessively. It is often argued that there are other ways of reducing cardiovascular disease, such as better diet and regular exercise. For your pie-and-chips addicted, couch potato this may be true, but what about healthier specimens?

In 2006, a group of researchers looked at the impact on the risk of heart attack of alcohol consumption by men with

---

7   Malinski M, Sesso H, Lopez-Jimenez F, Buring J, Gaziano J. Alcohol consumption and cardiovascular disease mortality in hypertensive men. Archives of Internal Medicine. 22 Mar 2004; 164(6):623-8

8   Ajani U, Gaziano J, Lotufo P, Liu S, Hennekens C, Buring J, Manson J. Alcohol consumption and risk of coronary heart disease by diabetes status. Circulation. 1 Aug 2000; 102(5):500-5

9   Szmitko P, Verma S. Red wine and you heart. Circulation. 18 Jan 2005; 111(2):e10-11

healthy lifestyles. All participants in the study had to be free of major illness, not overweight, not smoke, exercise daily and have a diet assessed as being in the better half of the male population. Despite all these positive health indicators, drinking alcohol still improved their chances of avoiding a heart attack.[10]

In the US an Alternative Healthy Eating Index has been put together by Harvard School of Public Health. It aims to improve on the US Department of Agriculture's Healthy Eating Index and at least one study has demonstrated that health outcomes are better for followers of the modified nutritional guidelines.[11] Many of the recommendations are what you would expect – eat plenty of fruit and vegetables, get plenty of fibre, limit intake of trans fat, etc. However, one criterion is conspicuously different from the US Department of Agriculture's guidelines. In calculating the Alternative Healthy Eating Index score, maximum points are given for drinking between about 2½ and 4½ UK units of alcohol per day for men and between 1 and 2½ UK units per day for women. It is encouraging that there are serious people that consider that moderate alcohol consumption not only does you no harm, but can add to a healthy lifestyle in combination with other sensible traits.

This should not come as any great surprise; many have thought this, particularly in relation to wine, for centuries. Much of the recent research in this area was stimulated by

10   Mukamal K, Chiuve S, Rimm E. Alcohol consumption and risk for coronary heart disease in men with healthy lifestyles. Archives of Internal Medicine. 23 October 2006; 166(19): 2145-50

11   McCullough M, Feskanich D, Stampfer M, Giovannucci E, Rimm E, Hu F, Spiegelman D, Hunter D, Colditz G, Willett W. Diet quality and major chronic disease risk in men and women: moving toward improved dietary guidance. American Journal of Clinical Nutrition. 2002; 76:1261-71

the 'French Paradox'. This was the finding that the French had much less coronary heart disease than populations in countries such as the UK despite having similarly fatty diets; the explanation being their regular, and not always so moderate, red wine drinking with meals.

Alcoholic beverages, consumed sensibly, seem to lower the risk of cardiovascular diseases in both those who have already developed risk factors and those who are currently healthy. For those already following all the usual good-health principles, moderate consumption of alcohol may be one of the few additional factors they can add to their lifestyle to maintain health.

13

Wine – the Prince of Drinks?

We have mentioned the 'French Paradox' a couple of times. The benefits of drinking attributed to the French are principally from wine drinking; more specifically, red wine drinking. Within Europe there is a general trend for southern countries' populations to drink wine, often with meals, and for more northerly countries' populations to drink beer and spirits, often not with meals. From a cardiovascular health perspective, the southerners outshine the northerners.

The divide between wine drinkers and beer or spirit drinkers is a matter of climate. This is not just because the Scandinavians and Russians need a shot of the hard stuff to warm themselves up but because they can make spirits and beer from cereal crops that grow at more northerly latitudes. In southern Europe the grape is the logical source for fermentation and even the spirits tend to be distilled from fermented grapes in the form of brandy, marc, grappa, etc.

So is one form of alcoholic beverage better for you than another? As we have already discovered with epidemiology, it is as difficult to get a definitive view as it is to get a straight answer from a politician. Things can be a little hazy; although hopefully not the wine in your glass.

Ecological studies, those looking at broad populations,

usually give the thumbs up for wine. But as already discussed, wine drinking is often linked to more southerly countries, at least in Europe. This raises questions over whether
wine is the beneficial factor or other characteristics of these
populations, such as eating a Mediterranean diet, which seems
to be one of the healthiest on the planet.

Many other epidemiological studies, although not all,
show that wine is better for cardiovascular health than beer
or spirits. For example, a 2002 meta-analysis concluded that
wine reduced the risk of cardiovascular events more than
beer.[1] One particular study from 1995 showed that those
who drank 1 to 5 glasses of wine a day had less than half
the likelihood of dying from cardiovascular disease as those
that did not drink wine, with beer showing a smaller benefit
and spirits an increased risk.[2] Another cohort study showed
reduced risk of ischemic stroke in men drinking red wine in
moderation, but not for beer or spirits drinkers.[3]

These benefits of wine, that appear to be distinct from
the cardiovascular benefits of alcohol, are put down to its
polyphenolic content. Polyphenols are found in the skins
and pips of grapes and, hence, find their way into wine during fermentation. Many polyphenols are potent antioxidants,
capable of scavenging free radicals. This antioxidant property seems to be key in lowering the risk of cardiovascular
disease. Atherosclerosis, a hardening and narrowing of the

1   Di Castelnuovo A, Rotondo S, Iacoviello L, Donati M, de Gaetano G. Meta-
analysis of wine and beer consumption in relation to vascular risk. Circulation. 2002;
105:2836-44

2   Gronbaek M, Deis A, Sorensen T, Becker U, Schnohr P, Jensen G. Mortality associated with moderate intakes of wine, beer, or spirits. BMJ. 6 May 1995; 310:1165-9

3   Mukamal K, Ascherio A, Mittleman M, Conigrave K, Camargo Jr C, Kawachi I et
al. Alcohol and risk for ischemic stroke in men: The role of drinking patterns and usual
beverage. Annals of Internal Medicine. 4 Jan 2005; 142(1):11-19

arteries caused by fatty deposits in the arterial wall, is the principal cause of heart attacks and ischemic strokes.[4] Whilst LDL (low density lipids or 'bad cholesterol') is known to play a major part in the development of atherosclerosis, it is only when LDL is oxidised that damage starts to occur. Wine polyphenols appear to inhibit the oxidation of LDL thereby lowering the risk of atherosclerosis and cardiovascular disease. This effect, together with inhibition of blood clotting, the relaxation of blood vessel walls, an increase in HDL (high density lipids or 'good cholesterol') and promotion of healthy blood vessel walls, has made polyphenols the subject of much scientific investigation.

Recent research has shown another possible mechanism by which wine polyphenols may lower the risk of cardiovascular disease. Moderate drinkers have been shown to have higher levels of particular fatty acids in their blood – marine omega-3 fatty acids – the ones usually associated with eating fish oils.[5,6] As a consequence, this mechanism is sometimes termed the 'fish-like effect of moderate drinking'. It is known that these fatty acids protect against coronary heart disease. Research is still inconclusive as to how much of this 'fish-like' effect is due to alcohol and how much is down to polyphenols, but indications are that wine produces the biggest effect. What a fishy bunch of molecules these polyphenols turn out to be!

---

4   Cordova A, Jackson L, Berke-Schlessel D, Sumpio B. The cardiovascular protective effect of red wine. Journal of the American College of Surgeons. Mar 2005; 200(3):428-39

5   di Giuseppe R, de Lorgeril M, Salen P, Laporte F, Di Castelnuova A, Krogh V et al. Alcohol consumption and n-3 polyunsaturated fatty acids in healthy men and women from 3 European populations. American Journal of Clinical Nutrition. 2009; 89:354-62

6   de Lorgeril M, Salen P, Martin J, Boucher F, de Leiris J. Interactions of wine drinking with omega-3 fatty acids in patients with coronary heart disease: a fish-like effect of moderate wine drinking. American Heart Journal. Jan 2008; 155:175-81

Incremental cardiovascular benefits, beyond what alcohol alone can offer, are not the only wonders that wine polyphenols exhibit. A number of these compounds are being studied as they help guard against various cancers. Resveratrol is probably the biggest celebrity in the wine bottle, having been declared a cancer chemopreventive agent in 1997.[7] A cancer chemopreventive agent is a substance that prevents, inhibits or delays the development of cancer. Resveratrol started the interest in grape polyphenols and is even available in dietary supplements. However, the antioxidant properties of many polyphenols make them candidates to help reduce cancer risk.

The body of knowledge on the cancer chemopreventive properties of the non-alcohol components of wine is building, but is far from settled. Some laboratory experiments, for example, show positive effects of these substances on cancer cells, but that is not the same as showing that drinking wine will have the same effect. Can it be shown that the concentration of a polyphenol, say resveratrol, being studied is similar in the laboratory experiment to that in the blood stream of someone who has just enjoyed a couple of glasses of Chianti? This will depend on a number of factors including the quantity of the polyphenol present in the wine and its bioavailability – how much is actually absorbed in the body and reaches the bloodstream. Nevertheless, positive results, together with some negative or neutral ones too, have been published across conditions such as cancer of the lung, colon, ovaries, prostate, stomach and even the female breast.

7   Jang M, Cai L, Udeani G, Slowing K, Thomas C, Beecher C et al. Cancer chemo-preventive activity of resveratrol, a natural product derived from grapes. Science. 10 Jan 1997; 275:218-20

More work needs to be done, but positive results across a number of cancer sites is encouraging.

Looking back at the J-shaped curves for total mortality, it was evident that much of the reduced risk of dying was due to the cardiovascular benefits of drinking alcohol in moderation. The rising part of the curve was largely due to increased cancers and violent deaths from heavier or binge drinking. For those that drink in moderation, the right-hand, heavier drinking end of the curve should not be that relevant. Nevertheless, there was no suggestion that drinking alcohol had any beneficial effect on cancer at any level of consumption.

This is where wine gets exciting. There are indications that with alcohol and polyphenols together, there may actually be some reduction in cancer risk for moderate drinkers. Wine, it seems, may be the ultimate cocktail. As already mentioned, research in this area is ongoing, but even back in the 1995 paper mentioned at the beginning of this chapter, there was evidence of a reduced risk of cancer for wine drinkers. Gronbaek and colleagues found that moderate wine drinkers, but not beer or spirits drinkers, not only had a decreased risk of dying from cardiovascular diseases but also from other causes. A substantial proportion of those 'other causes' is cancer, being the second highest cause of death in most western countries after cardiovascular diseases. So wine drinkers, overall, probably had a reduced risk of cancer. This finding was repeated in 2000 in a similar study based on a broader range of participants that extended the data from the

1995 study.[8] Time and further research will shed more light on which cancers are affected by drinking wine, but for those who are partial to fermented grape juice the cancer story may well have a positive theme.

The anti-alcohol lobby might jump in here to suggest that, whilst they do not doubt the benefit of an antioxidant rich diet, eating lots of fruit and vegetables is the answer not the alcohol 'contaminated' polyphenols in wine. We all know we should aim to eat a balanced diet, but as researchers Ursini and Sevanian noted, "Eating the usual amounts of fruit, vegetables, olive oil or beer can by no means achieve the intake of antioxidants found in two to three glasses of red wine."[9] In fact the prom queen of wine polyphenols, resveratrol, is not found in most fruit and vegetables that form a major part of human diet.[10]

Resveratrol could be taken as a food supplement, but this rather misses the point. Resveratrol is part of a food, wine, and it is important to recognise the interactions between different nutrients. Most studies show a benefit of wine; that enticing mix of alcohol and thousands of other compounds. The 'fish-like' effect of wine is an interesting example of interactions. There is no fish-oil in wine yet it can affect the level of marine omega-3 fatty acids in the blood stream. It can be attractive for some to assume that there must be another way of achieving the same benefits offered by moderate drinking via another route, but this is not at all straight

8   Gronbaek M, Becker U, Johansen D, Gottschau A, Schnohr P, Hein H et al. Type of alcohol consumed and mortality from all causes, coronary heart disease, and cancer. Annals of Internal Medicine. 19 Sep 2000; 133(6):411-9

9   Ursini F, Sevanian A. Wine polyphenols and optimal nutrition. Annals of the New York Academy of Sciences. 2002; 957:200-9. Publisher: John Wiley and Sons.

10   Bhat K, Pezzuto J. Cancer chemopreventive activity of resveratrol. Annals of the New York Academy of Sciences. 2002; 957:210-29

forward. For example, one researcher reported that in a study determining factors related to HDL levels, alcohol consumption had a greater positive effect than physical exercise.[11]

Looking at aspects of diet or foods in isolation can have drawbacks. Ursini and Sevanian mention this problem in relation to the high saturated fat, low heart disease 'French Paradox'. They suggest that it is not so paradoxical when looking at the French diet as a whole, in particular when the interaction with protective factors in wine are considered. They suggest that wine lowers the heart disease risk in populations that are exposed to the risks of a high-fat diet, but may have little benefit where that dietary risk does not exist.

In a similar way, is there any value in splitting out particular nutrients from wine to make a food supplement pill? If drinking wine, with its thousands of complex molecules, is efficacious, why not just drink wine?

It is evident that if polyphenols add the sparkle to elevate wine above other alcoholic beverages, the level of polyphenols in a wine must be critical. All wines are not equal; both the grape variety and wine making processes affect the level of polyphenols in wine. The big divide is red versus white. White wines are generally produced by pressing the grapes at harvest and then fermenting the juice. As a consequence, the grape skins and pips, that contain most of the polyphenolic compounds, are separated from the wine at an early stage leaving only low levels of polyphenols in the finished product.

Red wine involves fermenting the juice with the skins and pips, and sometimes some of the stalks too. This is

11   Ellison R. Balancing the risks and benefits of moderate drinking. Annals of the New York Academy of Science. 2002; 957:1-6

essential to get the red colour out of the skins but also extracts large quantities of polyphenolic compounds that provide the tastes of bitterness and astringency. The longer the skin and pips are left in contact with the juice the greater the extraction, particularly as the increasing alcohol level helps dissolve the polyphenolic compounds. These polyphenols are natural preservatives enabling red wine to last for long periods of time. Although the modern winemaker has many techniques at his or her disposal to help preserve the quality and life of wine, it is possible to make red wines with little human intervention. White wines, with fewer natural antioxidants to preserve them, will tend to need more intervention, such as larger additions of sulphur dioxide, itself a powerful antioxidant.

Oak aging of wines also adds tannins to wine. However these polyphenolic compounds are too large to be absorbed into the bloodstream and are, therefore, not thought to have a health impact except perhaps in the gut.

The result is that white wines typically have a fifth to a tenth of the level of polyphenols that red wines have and less than a tenth of the quantity of resveratrol. Rosé wines are nearer the white wine end of the scale than red. A few studies discriminate between red and white wine, with red wine showing benefits that white wine does not elicit. White wines contain low levels of polyphenols, but then so do many beers.

One of the major cardiovascular benefits of red wine over other alcoholic beverages is its antioxidant effect, inhibiting the oxidation of LDL. Alcohol alone appears to have an oxidising effect rather than the beneficial antioxidant

effect of polyphenols. For beverages containing alcohol
and polyphenols there is a tug-of-war as to which effect
wins out. In red wine, polyphenols seem to exert the greater
effect, providing the desired overall antioxidant property.[12]
With white wine and beer, which only contain low levels of
polyphenols, the overall antioxidant effect is small or possibly
negative.

Due to the way that epidemiological research into alcohol has developed, the precise data researchers might like is
not always to hand. Many studies were set up years ago to
provide a databank of details on diet, lifestyle, etc and information on the specific illnesses or causes of death suffered
by participants in succeeding years, but not with research
into alcohol or red wine specifically in mind. When the 'sick
quitter' hypothesis was put forward, much of the foregoing
data was not detailed enough to distinguish lifelong abstainers
from those who had given up alcohol later in life, perhaps
due to illness. Similarly, with an increasing interest in the type
of beverage rather than alcohol per se, the data on beverage
type is not always available. In particular, in most studies that
do permit a distinction between types of drink, the division is
typically wine, beer and spirits. This lacks any separation of
red and white wine, where white wine may well behave more
like beer than red wine given its similarly low level of polyphenolic compounds. Surprisingly, even a number of more
recent studies that look at beverage types fail to separate out
red and white wine.

One can hypothesise that this may be the reason why not

---

12   Cordova A, Jackson L, Berke-Schlessel D, Sumpio B. The cardiovascular protective effect of red wine. Journal of the American College of Surgeons. Mar 2005;
200(3):428-39

all studies show wine being more beneficial than other beverages. If there is a prince of drinks it is not wine in general, but polyphenol-rich, red wine, preferably made with a long maceration period when skins and pips are in contact with the juice. If research into 'wine' includes white wine, which may have no more polyphenols than many beers, this would dilute the apparent benefits of polyphenol-rich red wine, possibly to an extent that wine no longer shows up as being more beneficial than any other alcoholic beverage. Hopefully more research going forward will distinguish between red and white wine.

Even within the category of red wine there is a broad range of levels of polyphenolic compounds. The level can be affected by grape variety, where and how the grapes are grown and, of course, by the winemaker.

For example, flavonols, a class of polyphenol synthesised in the grape skin, increase with greater sunlight exposure. Undoubtedly the most impressive study I came across in my research for this book was a paper that demonstrated that more expensive Cabernet Sauvignon wines, expected to come from lower yielding vines with better sun exposure, had significantly higher levels of polyphenols. In the case of flavonols, levels were almost 4 times higher than in cheaper wines.[13] What fantastic work: surely the authors deserve a Nobel Prize! Now I have a justification for spending more money on a decent bottle of red wine; it is all about health. Higher price means higher polyphenolic levels, means greater antioxidant properties, means greater cardiovascular benefits,

13   Ritchey J, Waterhouse A. A standard red wine: monomeric phenolic analysis of commercial Cabernet Sauvignon wines. American Journal of Enology and Viticulture. 1999; 50(1):91-100

and possibly a lower risk of some cancers too! Normally I try to find corroborative research and delve more deeply into a new research finding. But in this case my drive for unbiased facts has dwindled; I don't want to complicate the picture. I am happy to take this research at face value, no questions asked. I will graciously accept that in the interests of my health I should buy more expensive red wine. I suspect others may unquestioningly accept this finding too!

14

A Broader Tonic

Discussion of drinking benefits naturally focuses on the heart and circulation as illness in these areas affects such a large proportion of the populations of the richer world. Yet the health enhancing effects of moderate consumption of alcohol, and sometimes red wine in particular, stretch to other chronic diseases. In this chapter, a number of these other illnesses are considered briefly. Not every piece of research points in the same direction; in many of these areas more research is needed to clarify the picture. However, let us start with a disease where researchers are almost entirely in agreement that alcohol is beneficial. That disease is type 2 diabetes mellitus.

DIABETES

Type 2 diabetes is a scourge of modern, wealthy societies. Unlike type 1 diabetes, it usually develops over time in adults and is largely a product of poor diet choice and the fact that modern living means many of us spend far too long sitting on our backsides. Consequently, improved diet and exercise are the first ports of call in trying to slow the tsunami of diabetes that now affects about 8% of Americans, 3.5% of the British and 6% of Australians. Drinking alcoholic beverages in moderation is one aspect of diet that can help prevent diabetes. In a meta-analysis of 13 studies, researchers found that moderate drinkers had almost a 30% lower risk of diabetes than non-drinkers.[1] This benefit was of a similar magnitude for men and women.

In a review paper covering 32 studies, researchers recorded that the benefit of moderate drinking was a reduction in the risk of diabetes of between 33% and 56% compared with non-drinkers.[2] In addition, amongst those with diabetes, moderate drinkers enjoyed a greatly reduced risk of coronary heart disease. This is important as diabetes is a risk factor for coronary health.

Insulin is produced within the pancreas and its level in the blood stream regulates the amount of glucose in the blood. Type 2 diabetes is caused by the cells of the body not responding properly to insulin, called a reduction in 'insulin sensitivity', or insufficient production of insulin. Consuming any alcoholic beverage appears to increase insulin sensitivity, and this is at least one mechanism by which the risk of diabetes is reduced through moderate drinking. It is thought that increased insulin sensitivity may be associated with cardiovascular benefits as well.[3]

DEMENTIA

With our aging populations in the western world, dementia is a growing problem. It usually starts as mild cognitive impair-

1   Carlsson S, Hammar N, Grill V. Alcohol consumption and type 2 diabetes. Diabetologia. 2005; 48:1051-54

2   Howard A, Arnsten J, Gourevitch M. Effect of alcohol consumption on diabetes mellitus. Annuals of Internal Medicine. 3 Feb 2004; 140(3):211-9

3   Lazarus R, Sparrow D, Weiss S. Alcohol intake and insulin levels. American Journal of Epidemiology. 1997; 145(10):909-16

ment before progressing to dementia in one of its forms, Alzheimer's disease being the most common. It not only afflicts the sufferer but also puts a huge strain on family and carers.

Around 20 years ago a meta-analysis concluded that there was no detrimental effect from alcohol consumption on the risk of dementia.[4] The same report hinted at a possible benefit of moderate drinking, but the results were not statistically significant. However, more recently, there have been a number of encouraging studies of the relationship between moderate drinking and dementia. A Rotterdam study showed an average 40% reduction in the risk of dementia for moderate drinkers, with a greater benefit for men than women.[5] A study of women only in the USA found a 20% reduction in the risk of cognitive impairment for moderate drinkers.[6]

As well as the indications that moderate drinking may lower the risk of dementia, there is evidence that it may slow or prevent the progression to dementia of those that already have mild cognitive impairment.[7]

The studies mentioned above either did not try to distinguish between types of alcoholic beverage or found no difference between wine, beer and spirits. However, two studies

4   Graves A, van Duijn C, Chandra V, Fratiglioni L, Heyman A, Jorm A et al. Alcohol and tobacco consumption as risk factors for Alzheimer's disease: a collaborative re-analysis of case-control studies. International Journal of Epidemiology. 1991; 20(2) (Suppl 2):S48-S57

5   Ruitenberg A, van Swieten J, Witteman J, Mehta K, van Duijn C, Hofman A, Breteler M. Alcohol consumption and risk of dementia: the Rotterdam Study. The Lancet. 26 Jan 2002; 359:281-6

6   Stampfer M, Kang J, Chen J, Cherry R, Grodstein F. Effects of moderate alcohol consumption on cognitive function in women. The New England Journal of Medicine. 20 Jan 2005; 352(3):245-53

7   Solfrizzi V, D'Introno A, Colacicco A, Capurso C, Del Parigi A, Baldassarre G et al. Alcohol consumption, mild cognitive impairment, and progression to dementia. Neurology. 22 May 2007; 68:1790-9

do show a marked benefit of wine over beer and spirits. A Canadian study showed a 50% reduction in dementia risk for wine drinkers, with beer and spirits still showing a benefit, albeit a statistically non-significant one.[8] Another research paper, this time from Copenhagen, showed a benefit for wine but not beer or spirits.[9] As with other areas of research into the chronic effects of alcohol consumption, few studies distinguish between red and white wine, potentially reducing the perceived benefits of red wine where any benefit is derived from the high polyphenol levels that are associated with red wine, but not white wine.

It is thought that oxidative stress may play a part in the development of dementia. If this is the case then antioxidants, such as polyphenols in red wine, might have a role in preventing dementia. It has been found that people consuming higher levels of flavonoids, powerful antioxidants found in tea, fruit, vegetables and red wine, have a much lower risk of dementia. A French study looked at flavonoid intake and the risk of dementia. It compared the two thirds of people consuming the most flavonoids with the lowest third and found that the group with higher flavonoid intake had half the chance of getting dementia.[10] On average, about one sixth of participants' flavonoid intake was from wine.

The position with dementia looks a little like that for cardiovascular disease. There is evidence to suggest that

8   Lindsay J, Laurin D, Verreault R, Hebert R, Helliwell B, Hill G, McDowell I. Risk factors for Alzheimer's disease: a prospective analysis from the Canadian study of health and aging. American Journal of Epidemiology. 2002; 156(5):445-53

9   Truelsen T, Thudium D, Gronbaek M. Amount and type of alcohol and risk or dementia. Neurology. Nov 2002; 59:1313-9

10   Commenges D, Scotet V, Renaud S, Jacqmin-Gadda H, Barberger-Gateau P, Dartigues J. Intake of flavonoids and risk of dementia. European Journal of Epidemiology. 2000; 16:357-63

all alcoholic beverages are beneficial in reducing the risk of dementia and progression from mild cognitive impairment to dementia. Then there is a second consideration that antioxidants may help prevent dementia, which would suggest that red wine can offer additional benefits, over alcohol alone, due to its high polyphenolic content.

OSTEOPOROSIS

Osteoporosis literally means 'porous bones' and refers to a decreased density in bones leading to a greater risk of fracture. It is estimated that 230,000 broken bones a year in the UK are a consequence of osteoporosis, with women being more than twice as likely as men to be affected. Some reduction in bone density is a natural part of aging, starting in middle age, and it is estimated that by age 75 about half the population has osteoporosis. However, earlier excess loss of bone density can occur in some people with women being particularly vulnerable post menopause. Osteoporosis increases the risk of fractures from even relatively minor bumps or falls.

As with so many health conditions, the effect of alcohol consumption depends on the quantity consumed. Heavy drinking may be a risk factor for osteoporosis and is a clear risk for fractures. Moderate drinking is far more beneficial. A recent review of studies into osteoporosis and hip fractures concluded that there is a J-shaped relationship between alcohol consumption and hip fracture risk with the lowest risk in those drinking up to about 2 standard drinks a day.[11]

---

11   Berg K, Kunins H, Jackson J, Nahvi S, Chaudhry A, Harris K et al. Association between alcohol consumption and both osteoporotic fracture and bone density. The American Journal of Medicine. May 2008; 121(5):406-18

Interestingly, the same review showed that bone density increased linearly with alcohol intake, at least at moderate consumption levels. Presumably the increased risk of hip fractures as drinking levels go up implies that increased bone density is insufficient to offset the risk of falling over more often when inebriated!

Yet again we see that overindulgence is bad for your health, but drinking alcoholic beverages in moderation is beneficial.

GALLSTONES

Gallstones are less common in moderate drinkers than abstainers and, it appears, heavier drinkers fair better too. A large prospective study of gallstone disease in women showed increasingly beneficial effects of alcohol even up to an intake exceeding 6 units a day.[12] In an earlier study, many of the same research team had found a similarly beneficial effect of alcohol consumption for men. There is a hint that wine may be more beneficial than beer or spirits, but all three seem to be quite efficacious.

AND THE OTHERS

There are suggestions of benefits in other areas too. The risk of renal dysfunction in male moderate drinkers[13] and kidney stones in wine drinkers[14] may be less than for non-drinkers.

---

12   Leitzmann M, Tsai C, Stampfer M, Rim E, Colditz G, Willett W, Giovannucci E. Alcohol consumption in relation to risk of cholecystectomy in women. American Journal of Clinical Nutrition. 2003; 78:339-47

13   Schaeffner E, Kurth T, de Jong P, Glynn R, Buring J, Gaziano J. Alcohol consumption and the risk of renal dysfunction in apparently healthy men. Archives of Internal Medicine. 9 May 2005; 165:1048-53

14   Curhan G, Willet W, Speizer F, Stampfer M. Beverage use and risk for kidney stones in women. Annals of Internal Medicine. 1 April 1998; 128(7):534-40

Prostate enlargement is one of the most common medical conditions in older men, causing frequent urination, but appears to benefit from alcohol consumption.[15] There may even be a beneficial relationship between alcohol consumption and rheumatoid arthritis.[16]

Many areas of health are being researched to see what impact, if any, drinking alcohol has on them. Unlike cardiovascular disease, many of these areas have not been researched in sufficient detail to draw clear-cut conclusions. Nevertheless, it is encouraging that a number of areas of health are giving rise to positive studies for those that consume alcohol in moderation.

Before finishing this chapter, it is worth taking a moment to comment on gout. To many, gout is the archetypal heavy-drinker's disease; not life-threatening like liver cirrhosis, but a common complaint of those who have lived well, perhaps a little too well. Certainly there is a strong and undeniable link between alcohol and gout. Gout is the cause of a sore big toe in many a heavy drinker. But even here, a blanket condemnation of alcoholic beverages may be unwarranted. There are suggestions that although beer and spirits may deserve some blame, wine might be an innocent bystander,[17] implicated merely by association.

15   Kristal A, Arnold K, Schenk J, Neuhouser M, Goodman P, Penson D, Thompson I. Dietary patterns, supplement use, and the risk of symptomatic benign prostatic hyperplasia: results from the prostate cancer prevention trial. American Journal of Epidemiology. 2008; 167(8):925-34

16   Kallberg H, Jacobsen S, Bengtsson C, Pedersen M, Padyukov L, Garred P et al. Alcohol consumption is associated with decreased risk of rheumatoid arthritis: results from two Scandinavian case-control studies. Annals of the Rheumatic Diseases. 2009; 68:222-7

17   Choi H, Curhan G. Beer, liquor, and wine consumption and serum uric acid level: the third national health and nutrition examination survey. Arthritis and Rheumatism. 15 Dec 2004; 51(6):1023-9

15

Breast Cancer

We have seen that drinking can be a contributory factor for a number of illnesses, including cancers of the oesophagus, mouth/pharynx and liver. Yet the evidence is that the majority of that risk falls on heavy drinkers. In addition, whilst these conditions should not be ignored, they are not the big killers. The percentage of deaths in England and Wales attributable to cancer of the oesophagus, mouth/pharynx and liver is 1.3%, 0.4% and 0.6% respectively.[1] Consequently a modest additional risk for these neoplasms only equates to a very small absolute additional risk of dying from cancer. Furthermore, there is always the possibility that further research might indicate that there is a threshold level of alcohol intake before any meaningful risk accrues for the genuine light or moderate drinker.

Cancer of the female breast is different. Deaths from breast cancer are about the same as from the three above-mentioned cancers put together and that, of course, is for women only. Comparing women with women, breast cancer accounts for 2.6 times more deaths than cancer of the oesophagus, mouth/pharynx and liver put together. But deaths

---

1   Mortality statistics, deaths registered in 2008. Office for National Statistics (UK) (www.statistics.gov.uk)

are only part of the story; many women now survive breast cancer, but still have to suffer the treatment – possibly even mastectomy. It is estimated that women in the developed world have around a one in 10 lifetime probability of being diagnosed with breast cancer. In the UK, some 45,000 women receive the bad news on breast cancer each year; it is the most common cancer in women.

Further bad news is that studies indicate that the increased alcohol-related risk of breast cancer starts at quite low levels of alcohol consumption; certainly within the bounds of what most people would consider moderate drinking. In 2002 a collaborative meta-analysis of 53 epidemiological studies, conducted from Oxford, showed an increased risk of 5.7% for every standard drink consumed every day of the week.[2] This study was remarkable in that the authors had access to the underlying data for all these studies, as opposed to just the published results, and covered about 80% of all the relevant information worldwide. A further meta-analysis in 2006 included 98 unique studies and came up with an increased risk per daily standard drink of 8%.[3] There could still be a threshold limit below which no harm accrues. However, given that 88% of the drinkers in the first-mentioned meta-analysis drank no more than 3 standard drinks per day and still showed an increased risk, the threshold level would presumably be very low.

Of course, the average increased risk derived from

2   Collaborative group on hormonal factors in breast cancer. Alcohol, tobacco and breast cancer – collaborative reanalysis of individual data from 53 epidemiological studies, including 58515 women with breast cancer and 95067 women without the disease. British Journal of Cancer. 2002; 87(11):1234-45

3   Key J, Hodgson S, Omar R, Jensen T, Thompson S, Boobis A et al. Meta-analysis of studies of alcohol and breast cancer with consideration of the methodological issues. Cancer Causes Control. 2006; 17:759-70

analysis of the myriad of individual studies is still small. For illustrative purposes, let us take the UK Government's sensible drinking guideline for women as a definition of moderate drinking. That guideline is to drink no more than 2 or 3 units per day; we will say 2½ units for this example. On that basis, the increased risk of breast cancer for moderate-drinking women would be around 14% to 20%. The Oxford study extrapolates this additional risk to mean that in the developed world 10.1 of every 100 moderate drinkers would get breast cancer over their lifetime compared with 8.8 of every 100 teetotallers.

I have gone into a little detail on breast cancer because it is the principal type of neoplasm that potentially presents a materially increased absolute risk for moderate drinkers. It is still necessary to balance this increased risk of breast cancer with the cardiovascular and other benefits of drinking in moderation. Nevertheless, no-one really wants to contemplate a material increase in the risk of cancer even if overall they should live longer. So there you have the cold facts; the average risk derived from dozens of studies. How you weigh them in your own mind is your decision. But before you start that process, there are some other details to consider that might alter your perspective.

I would not want anyone to accuse me as an author of dismissing the risk of breast cancer for moderate drinkers. Above, I have given the 'average' facts as accurately as I understand them. But please do not think this is cut and dried; far from it.

In the second meta-analysis mentioned above, Jane Key and colleagues first compared the risk of breast cancer for

drinkers (at any level) with abstainers. They found a significant increased risk. Yet of the 89 studies used in that calculation 29 found a lower risk for breast cancer! Put another way,
one third of all the studies they looked at considered alcohol
consumption to be protective in relation to breast cancer,
not a risk factor. This range of results from different studies
is politely termed heterogeneity in research circles. In more
colloquial terms, it means the results are all over the shop; we
don't really know what is going on!

Furthermore, Key et al found that different types of
study gave big differences in estimated risk. In case-control
studies, researchers investigate a particular characteristic (in
this case alcohol consumption) of a group of people (the
cases) that suffer from a particular disease (here, breast cancer). They then compare the prevalence of the characteristic
in a group of people without the disease under investigation
(the controls). It turns out that where these controls are
selected from affects the results. In studies that used patients
in hospital as controls the risk estimates were almost twice
that when controls were selected from the community at
large. In another large meta-analysis from 2001, researchers found the same problem.[4] Case-control studies with
community-based controls showed similar risk to cohort
studies, but where hospital-based controls were used the risk
estimates were 70% higher than cohort studies. This may all
sound a bit technical, but cohort studies, which follow a large
group of people over time to see who develops a disease,
are prone to less bias than case-control studies. Therefore,

4   Ellison R, Zhang Y, McLennan C, Rothman K. Exploring the relation of alcohol
consumption to risk of breast cancer. American Journal of Epidemiology. 2001;
154(8):740-7

if using hospital-based controls shows higher risks but using community-based controls looks in line with cohort studies, one has to question whether the studies with hospital-based controls are as reliable. These studies using hospital-based controls may exaggerate the risks. Consequently, the 'average' risks calculated by meta-analysis may well be slightly over-stated. When the estimated risks of breast cancer for moderate drinkers are modest to begin with, even a small over-statement of the risk could affect women's perspective of how risky moderate drinking really is.

Returning to the reported risk figures again, it is worth noting that these risk estimates cover all drinkers at a particular average level of alcohol consumption. We have already noted that drinking 2 or 3 units every day is not the same as a 20-unit binge at the weekend. This aspect of alcohol and breast cancer does not seem to have been extensively researched. When dealing with average risks, any behaviour we would not consider as 'moderate drinking' that has a higher risk, effectively lowers the real risk for the genuine moderate drinkers.

The significant amount of variation between studies on the link between alcohol and breast cancer looks likely to be caused by 'effect modification'. What this would mean is that alcohol does have an adverse effect on breast cancer risk but mainly, or perhaps only, if other conditions apply. If those other conditions are absent the risk from alcohol would be limited or non-existent. This would explain the different study results. The problem is we are still not sure what these interacting factors are, although many possibilities have been proposed. For example, there are a number of studies that show that alcohol use combined with hormone replacement therapy raises breast cancer risk substantially more than either would seem to do so on its own. Similarly, alcohol may increase risks more in those with a family history of breast cancer.[5]

One particular area of interest is levels of folate in the diet. Folate is a B vitamin found in many vegetables, particularly the green ones, citrus fruits and juices, whole grain foods, beans, berries and meats. It has a number of functions in the body, including a role in the production of RNA and DNA, which are involved in cell replication. Although there is not necessarily a direct protective effect of folate on breast cancer risk, it does appear to mitigate the additional risk from consuming alcohol. It is notable that the highest risk from drinking alcohol pertains to those that have low folate levels in their diets. Research shows that the benefits of adequate folate intake in drinkers can be very substantial.[6] Interestingly, female folate intakes in the UK tend to decrease with younger age. Therefore, the concerns about more young women and girls drinking too much may be exacerbated as far as breast cancer risk is concerned by inadequate folate intake.

Another bright spot on the research canvas, this time unrelated to alcohol intake, is the sunshine vitamin – vitamin D. Two recent studies, one a meta-analysis,[7] concluded that high-

5   Vachon C, Cerhan J, Vierkant R, Sellers T. Investigation of an interaction of alcohol intake and family history on breast cancer in the Minnesota breast cancer family study. Cancer. 15 July 2001; 92(2):240-8

6   Baglietto L, English D, Gertig D, Hopper J, Giles G. Does dietary folate intake modify effect of alcohol consumption on breast cancer risk? Prospective cohort study. BMJ. 8 Oct 2005; 331(7520):807

7   Gissel T, Rejnmark L, Mosekilde L, Vestergaard P. Intake of vitamin D and risk of breast cancer – a meta-analysis. Journal of Steroid Biochemistry and Molecular Biology. 2008; 111:195-9

er intakes of vitamin D might significantly reduce the risk of breast cancer.[8] At very high intakes, that might be difficult to attain, vitamin D was shown to reduce the risk of breast cancer by about 50%. However, even at more moderate levels, a protective effect was evident. There is no suggestion of an interaction with alcohol, but if you are worried about increasing your breast cancer risk through drinking, it may be sensible to take other steps to mitigate that risk. Increasing your vitamin D intake is one possibility.

This only touches on the numerous areas that may affect breast cancer risk. Breast cancer covers a range of tumour types and the list of potential risk factors in research papers is enormous: smoking, low physical activity, being overweight, low intake of fruit and vegetables, high fat intake, older at first childbirth, early menarche, having relatives with breast cancer, night work, use of hormone replacement therapy, late menopause, radiation exposure, high socio-economic status, using oral contraceptives, using hair dyes, being single, being Jewish, etc, etc.

So what does this all mean? There appear to be three implications of this rather inconclusive research.

Keep a look out for further study findings in relation to alcohol consumption and breast cancer. It may be that with further research, some of the links between alcohol, breast cancer and interacting factors will become a little clearer.

From a policy point of view, the current estimates of additional breast cancer risk from drinking provide another reason for being more cautious on sensible drinking guide-

8   Garland C, Gorham E, Mohr S, Grant W, Giovannucci E, Lipkin M et al. Vitamin D and prevention of breast cancer: pooled analysis. Journal of Steroid Biochemistry and Molecular Biology. 2007; 103:708-11

lines for women than for men. Alcohol spreads throughout the human body in all the cells containing water; muscle tissue contains about 7 times more water than body fat. As women are on average smaller than men and have a higher proportion of body fat, their total body water is less than men leading to more elevated alcohol levels in the blood for a given intake of alcohol. Consequently, guidelines for women are usually lower than for men. The potential, modest increased risk of breast cancer for moderate drinking women, seems to confirm that a lower guide for women is merited.

Finally, maintaining a balanced diet seems all the more sensible as we do not want to be deficient in any nutrient, particularly if we are not entirely sure which ones we need to prevent each potential disease or problem. For breast cancer, current research suggests that maintaining folate and vitamin D levels may be particularly important.

16

The Moral Dimension

By this stage of the book, I hope that any misgivings you
may have had that moderate consumption of alcohol may be
damaging your health are fading. However, for some there
may be a guilty feeling about drinking alcohol at all. Many
churches have had prohibitionary tendencies or, at least,
strong temperance teachings. Not that I would criticise temperance in alcohol consumption; surely that is not dissimilar
to drinking in moderation. But for some, drinking alcohol,
if not sin itself, is the first step to all kinds of evil and despi-
cable behaviour.

Whilst trying to find the source of a quotation about
wine on the internet, I stumbled across an American religious
discussion website. The heated debate was about whether
Jesus drank wine or, as the main protagonist maintained,
drank grape juice instead. This debater was determined that
Jesus would not drink anything as sinful as wine. She maintained that 'wine', sometimes translated 'fruit of the vine',
was grape juice, unfermented.

This is pretty extreme as anti-alcohol interpretations
of the Bible go, but it does show how people can convince
themselves that alcohol is bad and abstaining from alcohol is
virtuous. Yet this position is difficult to maintain. It is aston-

ishing that any churchgoers can believe that wine, and other alcoholic beverages, are bad per se. Of course alcohol can be abused, but all alcohol and all drinkers are not evil.

Most are familiar with the Biblical account that Jesus' first miracle was to turn large quantities of water into large quantities of wine at a wedding feast – a strange thing to do if drinking alcohol is wicked. Just in case someone might think this was 'fruit of the vine' unfermented, it is recorded that the wine was taken to the Master of the Feast who commented that it was rather good stuff. It is difficult to imagine that he would have been too excited about six huge pots of grape juice!

Similarly, it is impossible to commemorate the Lord's Supper without drinking wine. Jesus' last meal with his disciples was a celebration of the Jewish Passover, which falls in the spring. There could not have been any grapes available from which to make grape juice at that time of year. Unless pasteurisation and Tetrapak were invented rather earlier that usually assumed, the only grape juice around in the spring would have either turned to undrinkable vinegar or fermented into wine. Therefore, drinking 'wine' or the 'fruit of the vine' meant drinking fermented grape juice! If one wished to be gentle with the internet debater who was determined that Jesus did not drink wine, one could perhaps mollify her with Lord Soper's view that, "Wine is the juice of the grape gone bad." Call it bad grape juice or wine, it would certainly have contained alcohol.

The Bible does warn against drunkenness or mixing with drunkards. Those administering the law should be sober (sober as a judge) and various groups of Christians are not to be "given to much wine". Yet wine is mentioned many times as an agricultural blessing, along with ample wheat and olive oil.

Balance seems the sensible course, not prohibition. It reminds me of the story of a young man that went to his local clergyman and asked, "Sir, what can I do to live forever?"

The minister looked at the young man and said sombrely, "Give up alcohol, give up smoking, give up sex, give up chocolate, give up red meat, don't listen to music and don't drive fast cars."

The young man replied questioningly, "Will giving up all those things really mean that I will live forever?"

The clergyman fixed his gaze on the young man and said, "No son, it won't make you live forever, but it will feel like it!"

Nowadays, you will regularly hear reports that alcohol does more harm than illicit drugs. Regardless of how these comparisons are reached and the validity of the measurement, there is a world of difference between alcohol and illicit drugs. It is a bit like comparing a screwdriver and a dagger. A screwdriver is a useful tool, but one that can be used as a lethal weapon; just as lethal as a dagger. But its primary purpose is as a tool. A dagger on the other hand is a weapon designed for injuring or killing; it has no other purpose.

Alcohol is a normal part of the human diet, forms part of a number of enjoyable and convivial beverages, but can cause huge damage when misused. Illicit drugs have no positive purpose, other than possibly in the area of pain relief, and therefore are more like a dagger than a screwdriver. Of course, I have taken the view that alcohol is a food; part of a normal diet. I think history shows that is the case, even if some now see it as 'just another drug' or toxic substance. I side with Paracelsus, a 16th century German physician who wrote, "Whether wine is a nourishment, medicine or poison, is a matter of dosage." Keep drinking in moderation; treat alcohol as a food.

17

Policy, Politics & Propaganda

Many politicians and health practitioners are seriously concerned about the problems alcohol is causing. For example,
in the UK, mortality from liver disease, regarded as a barom-
eter of alcohol-related ill health, has increased more than
fivefold since 1970 in people under 65 years of age and is still
rising.[1]

In the executive summary of the UK Government's
2007 alcohol strategy paper "Safe Sensible Social" it states in
big, bold, red letters, "80% of people think that more should
be done to tackle the level of alcohol abuse in society."[2] I
am fully in agreement with the 80%. But you may be thinking, why discuss alcohol policy in a book about moderate
drinking? Genuine moderate drinkers do not contribute in
any significant way to the massive increase in liver disease,
the stream of alcohol-related injuries on a Saturday evening
or the overall cost burden on the National Health Service of
alcohol-related medical conditions. Policy matters, because
many of the messages and actions being promoted to reduce

1   UK House of Commons Health Committee. Alcohol, first report of session
2009-10. 8 January 2010. pp5, 29-30

2   UK Department of Health, Home Office, etc. Safe. Sensible. Social. The next steps
in the National Alcohol Strategy. Executive summary p5. 5 June 2007. Reproduced
under the terms of the Click-Use Licence.

alcohol-related harm will affect all drinkers, regardless of whether their drinking is sensible or excessive.

Two trends seem to be conspiring against a rational discussion of alcohol problems. The first trend is not isolated to alcohol policy; it seems to be permeating a number of areas where scientific research is mingled with politics to arrive at policy. This trend is the exaggeration, distortion and selective use of statistics to bolster the case for a particular policy. Despite there often being genuine underlying issues that need addressing, it seems many policymakers see the need to frighten the general public into accepting a new policy. The second trend is to paint alcohol as bad in all circumstances, rather than concentrating on alcohol misuse. Below are some examples of these trends and how they muddy the facts.

SELECTIVE USE OF STATISTICS

The UK Government's Safe Sensible Social paper estimates that excessive alcohol consumption is associated with between 15,000 and 22,000 premature deaths annually. This is a big number. Yet it fails to mention in the same section that the protective effect of alcohol against coronary heart disease and stroke is thought to prevent up to 22,000 deaths annually; that is in another section 10 pages away. Overall, the impact is at worst neutral. Clearly it is a sound objective to try to reduce the deaths caused whilst maintaining the deaths prevented, but one cannot read those figures together and see alcohol as universally bad. Presented in isolation, to the casual reader, the deaths caused figure looks horrifying.

Similar assessments in Australia and Canada have shown

that alcohol prevents more deaths than it causes.[3,4] In New Zealand, the results showed deaths caused numbering more than deaths prevented, but only by about 6%.[5] All these figures are estimates and different studies give different results, sometimes varying by multiples of two or three times the figure in other studies purporting to calculate the same thing. Mathematical models of this type depend entirely on the assumptions made and are only educated guesses at best. Nevertheless, in many developed countries, alcohol seems to be neutral on the death rate. Alcohol, overall, is not the killer-scourge that is oft depicted, even when all the alcohol abuse is taken into account, and we know that for moderate drinkers the benefits can be significant.

If the anti-alcohol advocates can be persuaded to admit that the net position is relatively neutral, their next trick is to change the definition of death; yes, really. Instead of deaths caused or prevented they move to number of years of life lost or gained. This is an estimate of the number of additional years people would have lived had they not died from alcohol-related causes, or the number of additional years people live because alcohol has helped prevent earlier death. They do this because lives saved through a reduction in heart disease tend to come later in life whereas drink-related accidents are often in younger people. This really is quite cynical. Are we as a society willing to accept that a life

3   Ridolfo B, Stevenson C. The quantification of drug-caused mortality and morbidity in Australia, 1998. Australian Institute of Health and Welfare, Canberra. Feb 2001

4   Single E, Robson L, Rehm J, Xi X. Morbidity and mortality attributable to alcohol, tobacco, and illicit drug use in Canada. American Journal of Public Health. Mar 1999; 89(3): 385-90

5   Connor J, Broad J, Rehm J, Hoorn S, Jackson R. The burden of death, disease, and disability due to alcohol in New Zealand. The New Zealand Medical Journal. 15 Apr 2005; 118(1213): 1-12

is worth less in old age than in middle age or youth? I hope not. Yes, the potential economic contribution of a young person is higher than that of an older person, but if that were how life was valued there would not only be people trying to encourage voluntary euthanasia, there would be legislation for involuntary euthanasia at pension age!

Imagine the defence lawyer of some young thug that has just robbed and murdered an octogenarian.

"The jury must understand that the deceased had been drawing a pension for two decades and in recent years had been in hospital on a number of occasions for lengthy and expensive procedures. Therefore, although the defendant is a vile good-for-nothing, on this occasion he should actually be commended for the economic benefit he has brought to the country!"

A selective use of statistics is often applied to the costs of alcohol misuse. For the year 2000/1, in England, it is estimated that alcohol misuse cost the NHS between £1.4 billion and £1.7 billion, lost workplace productivity related to alcohol cost £5.2 to £6.4 billion and alcohol-related crime and anti-social behaviour cost £7.3 billion.[6] The total is an enormous £13.9 to £15.4 billion per year; quite staggering if read in isolation. Clearly these costs should be reduced where possible, but one must not forget the revenue that alcohol brings into Her Majesty's Treasury. Duties and VAT on alcohol sales for 2000/1 brought in around £10 billion alone,[7]

---

6   The Information Centre (UK National Health Service). Statistics on Alcohol: England 2007 pp77-78, quoting from UK Cabinet Office Strategy Unit. Alcohol Misuse: How much does it cost? Sep 2003.

7   The Information Centre. Statistics on Alcohol: England 2006 p74 – data prorated by population (duty and VAT data is for UK; more than 50% of costs in footnote 6 are for England and Wales with the remainder for England only)

about two thirds of the estimated costs. One must also factor in that over a million people are employed in hotels, pubs, bars, nightclubs and restaurants in the UK where alcohol is a key part of the business; just think of all the payroll taxes from that, not to mention corporation tax!

Scientific advice can also be manipulated. Drinking, even moderately, during pregnancy is a sensitive area and I have every sympathy with women that change all kinds of diet and other behaviours during pregnancy, as a precaution, to protect the unborn child. But does the fact that an issue needs to be treated carefully warrant turning evidence upside down?

The Safe Sensible Social Government paper provides an astonishing example of how facts and figures can be manipulated such that the final presentation of a concept is unrecognisable from the underlying data. In 2005, the Department of Health commissioned a review of the effects of low to moderate alcohol consumption in pregnancy. The Government paper states the review's finding as:

"...low to moderate consumption during pregnancy was not found to have any adverse effects on the baby." [8]

The paper goes on to say that the Government "decided to strengthen the wording of the advice to women". The revised wording became:

"As a general rule, pregnant women or women trying to conceive should

---

8   UK Department of Health, Home Office, etc. Safe. Sensible. Social. The next steps in the National Alcohol Strategy. pp35-36. 5 June 2007. Reproduced under the terms of the Click-Use Licence.

avoid drinking alcohol. If they do choose to drink, to protect the baby they should not drink more that 1 to 2 units of alcohol once or twice a week and should not get drunk."

The paper then says that this advice can be summarised (for labelling purposes on bottles of alcohol, for example) as:

"Avoid alcohol while pregnant or trying to conceive."

It is staggering that a Government paper can contend that there is any linkage between its advice and the underlying research when the research finding is turned on its head. The UK Government has taken the research finding that there is not "any adverse effects on the baby" from low to moderate drinking and transformed it into the advice "avoid alcohol while pregnant".

PAINTING ALL ALCOHOL AS BAD

The alcohol debate is not always what it seems. Whilst I have read numerous studies showing the benefits of moderate alcohol consumption, I have also seen that many involved in the alcohol debate disapprove of all drinking; they want everyone to drink less. To that end, as illustrated by the examples above, the anti-alcohol advocates are happy to present facts and figures such that alcohol is always presented in a bad light. For many, it seems the aim is to make alcohol look harmful in all cases, not just in those situations where abuse is involved.

Sometimes, this total lack of tolerance for any level of drinking can be stark. The UK House of Commons Select

Committee on Health produced a report on alcohol, having taken evidence from a wide range of interested parties. They report that the Chief Medical Officer informed them that there were no safe limits of drinking and another witness, a public health consultant, stated that, "...the risks in relation to harm are pretty well monotonic or linear meaning that the risk starts at zero and it goes upwards."[9]

It is difficult to understand how these fiercely anti-alcohol pronouncements can be squared with the bulk of epidemiological research into alcohol. As has been described earlier in this book, the overall risks to life from consuming alcohol are U or J-shaped. Light and moderate drinkers fare better than those that do not drink at all. The balance of risks from drinking does not go up from zero; it goes down. It only rises again with heavier drinking. As far as anti-social behaviour and injuries are concerned, they are linked to intoxication, which is not a likely consequence of light or moderate drinking. Even in specific disease areas such as cancer, the evidence for an increased risk at a light to moderate level of drinking is not strong.

At this point you may be wondering why the anti-alcohol advocates, including many politicians, want to paint alcohol as an outright evil and get us all to drink less rather than have a more balanced debate about problem drinkers. Well there is a reason. Many in the anti-alcohol lobby are believers in the 'whole population theory' and see its application as the only way to reduce problem drinking. This theory holds that the number of problem drinkers in a society is directly linked to

9   UK House of Commons Health Committee. Alcohol, first report of session 2009-10. 8 January 2010. pp22, 27. Parliamentary material is reproduced with the permission of the Controller of HMSO on behalf of Parliament.

the average level of consumption in that society – and there are a number of studies that support this view. However, although lowering everyone's drinking level may well reduce alcohol-related harm in heavier drinkers, it does not make moderate drinking bad.

At the beginning of this book I quoted the wise words of Abraham Lincoln: "It has long been recognised that the problems with alcohol relate not to the use of a bad thing, but to the abuse of a good thing." It now appears that many in positions to guide alcohol policy are more inclined to believe that alcohol is an altogether bad substance; if you must drink at all, drink as little as possible. I suspect Abraham Lincoln's view will better stand the test of time.

THE EFFECTS ON ALCOHOL POLICY

For some years now, we seem to have been deluged with bad news about alcohol. It was as if we were being softened up for major policy shifts on drinking. The trends of exaggeration and vilification of alcohol in all circumstances are bound to start to affect public opinion. If the public can be persuaded to think that everything about alcohol is bad, they may be more willing to accept unpleasant prescriptions.

It appears that those unpleasant prescriptions are starting to be voiced more forcefully. Those that believe you tackle alcohol abuse by pressuring everyone to drink less maintain that the principal way to reduce alcohol consumption is to make it more expensive. In 2009, the Scottish Parliament proposed introducing a minimum price per unit of alcohol. Similarly, the Chief Medical Officer for England recommended setting a minimum price and has been joined

by the National Institute for Health and Clinical Excel-
lence – NICE. The House of Commons Select Committee
on Health has called for a combination of minimum unit
pricing and increased duty rates, particularly on spirits. By
their own figures, they wish to see the duty on spirits more
than double.[10] At the time of their first report, the tax (duty
plus VAT) on a standard 70cl bottle of 40% ABV spirits (eg
whisky, brandy, vodka, gin, rum) was a minimum of £7.45.
If the House of Commons Select Committee on Health had
its way, the tax would increase to a minimum of about £16.39
per bottle. If minimum unit pricing was adopted at 50p per
unit, the minimum price of a bottle of 14% wine would be
£5.25. It is not difficult to believe that raising the price of
alcohol would have an effect on how much people drink.
Clearly, if the price goes up overall consumption is likely to
decrease with the greatest impact on those that are less well
off. But is that an acceptable way to tackle the problem? It
is the class detention approach to trying to solve a problem;
two or three kids are messing around at the back of the class
so the teacher puts the whole class in detention.

   You cannot blame the anti-alcohol advocates for trying
to reduce alcohol abuse: alcohol can and does contribute
to many diseases and social ills. Impatience with a lack of
improvement in the situation is also understandable; current policies do not seem to be stemming the tide. By any
measure alcohol abuse is still the preserve of a minority, but
that minority is significant and growing. But is it balanced, is
it fair, is it reasonable to penalise the sensible, law-abiding,
moderate drinkers along with those that are a danger to

---

10   UK House of Commons Health Committee. Alcohol, first report of session
2009-10. 8 January 2010. p128

themselves and the broader society? There is something objectionable to the approach that says, let us restrict everyone's behaviour because of the irresponsible actions of a minority.

Yet there is another reason why it is inappropriate to pursue a blanket 'reduce all alcohol consumption' policy. It comes back to those U and J-shaped curves. It is only appropriate to reduce everyone's drinking if alcohol consumption is bad at all levels; we have seen that that is not what research shows. Alcohol policy should, therefore, seek to curb excessive consumption as reducing light or moderate consumption may actually put those drinkers in a worse situation. Perhaps policymakers should be reminded of what Thomas Jefferson said on the subject of taxing wine, "It is a tax on the health of our citizens." You can understand the debate over whether or not non-drinkers should be encouraged to drink in moderation to reduce their risk of cardiovascular disease. There is always the possibility that when some people start drinking they may be unable to control their new drinking and become addicted to alcohol with the disastrous consequences that would entail. However, it is more difficult to justify persuading stable, moderate drinkers that they should decrease their drinking and possibly decrease the health benefits they are gaining from their moderate drinking. Their current, stable drinking demonstrates that they are quite capable of maintaining their drinking at beneficial levels.

This book does not pretend to try to address the many problems that undoubtedly are caused or inflamed by alcohol misuse. However, we need to deal with the real problems, not the moderate drinkers that are minding their own business and probably minding their health too. Penalising all drinkers, through policies such as putting up the price of drink, does not seem balanced. This type of blanket approach looks like a failure of policy imagination to find a solution that targets those that need targeting.

18

Complex Yet Simple

Wow, there is a lot of it – enough to drown in! No I don't
mean alcohol, but all the research into its effects on human
health. If you search for published papers with 'alcohol'
in the title on PubMed,[1] a leading database of biomedical
research, there are more than 50,000 entries. Not all relate to
the consumption of alcohol, but thousands do. Add to that
the reports on alcohol from governments around the world
and the long list of organisations that publish information
about drinking and you start to see the scale of the effort
that has gone into understanding the health consequences of
alcohol consumption.

In researching this book I read many research papers
and followed trails through the lists of references to more
material, and so on; it was never-ending. I have not read
it all; I doubt anyone could. I hope, however, that I have
read many of the important papers and reports produced by
scientists, non-governmental organisations and governments.
The latter have the man-power to complete more exhaustive
literature reviews than any one individual could manage. I
noted that in the 10th Special Report to the US Congress on

Alcohol and Health,[2] prepared by the National Institute on
Alcohol Abuse and Alcoholism, that there were 40 people
that contributed to the report, a further 57 peer reviewers
and 11 people on the editorial board. As the foreword to the
report notes:

"The breadth and scope of alcohol research has grown so tremendously
that summarizing the total body of alcohol research in one document
is no longer manageable; so we have chosen to present the findings from
alcohol research in a new way – to summarize what is known in a par-
ticular area and to describe in greater detail significant research findings
that have been reported since the Ninth Special Report."

If you are thinking of taking a look at this 'slimmed
down summary', bear in mind it still runs to more than 450
pages!

So where has all this research and effort brought us?
The answer is that we know much more, but the complex
nature of the alcohol and health question has also become
more apparent. Many of the epidemiological studies have
shown associations with a decrease in this disease and an increase in another. Unfortunately, when groups of studies are
compared, the divergence in results is often great, pointing to
complexities and other issues we do not yet understand.

Part of this is the nature of these studies. When consid-
ering alcohol, two types of study predominate. Prospective
cohort studies take a group of people, record information
about them and then follow them over a period of time to
see who develops a particular disease or dies of a particular

2   pubs.niaaa.nih.gov/publications/10report/intro.pdf

cause. The follow-up periods can be in decades as chronic diseases often take a long time to develop. The second broad type of study is the case-control study where individuals that have a particular disease are selected and their histories are compared with a control group that does not have the disease to try to discover why the groups are different.

The problem is that so many other factors can affect the results. These other issues, often not well understood, are said to 'confound' the results if they are correlated to the consumption of alcohol and to the disease being considered; put in plain English, they mess it all up. If individual confounders have been identified an allowance can be made for them in the calculations, but one can never be sure that all confounders are known.

Greater complexity arises where effect modification occurs, as looks likely with the relationship between alcohol and breast cancer. Effect modification means that alcohol does have an effect on a particular disease but mainly, or possibly only, if other factors are present.

The 'gold standard' of medical study techniques is the double-blind, randomised controlled trial; these studies should provide more reliable conclusions. Participants in these studies are randomly assigned to the group that receives the substance under investigation (here alcohol) or the control group that does not receive it. The double-blind means that neither group knows whether they are receiving the real thing or just a placebo, nor do those directly administering the treatment as the treatments are coded; only those organising the trial know who is getting what. Unfortunately, with alcohol consumption, this route is beset with problems. For

starters, the double-blind is unlikely to work. I doubt many
participants would fail to notice the difference between a
glass of wine and a glass of water. Then you have to have
a sufficiently large group of willing participants that will
stick to the intake level of alcohol to which they have been
assigned for several years. Finally, for heavier drinking categories of participants there is an ethical issue over exposing
them to something that is expected to cause negative health
effects. Perhaps there would be plenty of volunteers for the
permanently sozzled category, but in these trials you do not
get to choose your dose!

As confounders, effect modification factors and other
complications are better understood they can be allowed for
in the studies. Complexities of the apparent beneficial effects of alcohol on cardiovascular disease are perhaps better
understood than in some areas because this effect of alcohol
has been researched for a long time. Other diseases are not
so well researched.

With cardiovascular disease, study design was an issue.
Allowing for the 'sick quitter' has reduced the measured
health difference between drinkers and abstainers. I hope
effort will be put into finding confounders and improving
study design where negative health effects of alcohol are
found as well as for diseases showing benefits. It must be
possible that the magnitude of some of these negative effects
might change when currently unrecognised confounders or
effect modification factors are eliminated, such as dietary
deficiencies. Similarly, improvements to study design might
help refine results as it did for cardiovascular health. As we
saw in chapter 15, a whole range of possible risk factors have

been put forward by researchers for breast cancer. Only time will tell how many of these, or yet undiscovered factors, will eventually be shown to be confounding or effect modification factors for breast cancer risk and alcohol consumption, but it would be surprising if some new complexities were not discovered.

It would also be helpful to see more analysis of risks for low to moderate drinkers, separate from heavy drinkers. When a link between heavy drinking and a particular disease becomes apparent, we should be careful about jumping to conclusions regarding what this tells us about the risk for moderate drinkers. Often a straight line or curve is fitted to the data across all levels of alcohol consumption leading to the conclusion that risk starts from the first drop of alcohol imbibed. The data for heavy drinkers pull the risk curves upwards; if researchers looked only at data for moderate drinking, would they still find the same risks?

In addition to the epidemiological studies there is all the laboratory research into how alcohol might cause these suspected benefits or problems with specific diseases. As discussed in an earlier chapter, one of the reasons why the benefit to cardiovascular disease is compelling is the fact that scientists have discovered a number of ways in which alcohol can have a positive health effect in this area – increasing good cholesterol, making blood clot less readily, etc. These processes are called biologically plausible mechanisms and, when coupled with strong epidemiological data, create a persuasive case for believing that a genuine positive or negative effect exists. Where the epidemiological data shows an effect but a biologically plausible mechanism is not known, it is best to be a bit sceptical and wait to see if the laboratory researchers can substantiate the epidemiological hypothesis.

To further complicate the issue, it appears that the pattern of drinking is also important. In particular, heavy drinking sessions tend to negate any benefits or increase risks. Binge drinking appears to be a problem although not even all the data in this area is consistent. Add to that the potential differences between types of alcoholic drink and the picture of how alcohol affects disease does appear pretty convoluted.

With all these complications it can be difficult for epidemiological studies to draw clear conclusions. For example, the graphs below are the type of results you might get from a meta-analysis of the effects of alcohol on a particular condition. The data in Fig 1 would probably lead researchers to conclude that this represents a straight line relationship, as the added trend line indicates. Similarly, the data in Fig 2 would probably be represented by a J-curve as shown. Yet, as you can see from the scatter plots of the individual results,

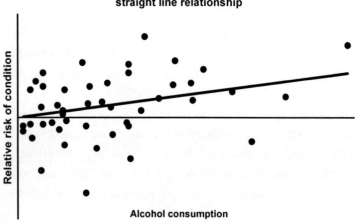

Fig 1. Illustrative example of meta-analysis results: straight line relationship

Relative risk of condition

Alcohol consumption

it is not immediately obvious to the naked eye that these two
sets of data represent straight line and J-shaped relationships.
This illustrates how data can appear dispersed and that statistical methods are often needed to interpret epidemiological
results.

Broader research into chronic diseases throws up further
complications. Some diseases seem to be linked to early
development – even to birth weight, not that there is much
you can do about you own birth weight. Mental outlook also
appears to impact physical health. Increased research does
bring better understanding but also makes clear how intricate
we humans are.

Over the last century or so, western lifestyles have
changed enormously. Childhood deaths have decreased
dramatically, as have deaths from infectious diseases, and we
are living longer. On the other hand, the rise in degenerative
diseases has been equally dramatic; cardiovascular disease
and cancers are the major killers today. If you are looking for

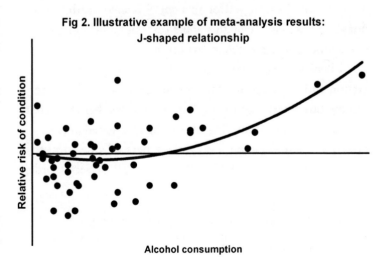

**Fig 2. Illustrative example of meta-analysis results:
J-shaped relationship**

Relative risk of condition

Alcohol consumption

a cause for these 'new' diseases, the modern processed-food
diet and sedentary lifestyle look much more likely culprits
than moderate alcohol consumption. Alcohol has been consumed for thousands of years. Highly processed food, often
nutritionally deficient, comprising manufactured fats, high
sugar levels, high salt and low fibre, have only been widely
consumed during the recent, rapid development of the
western world. This book is not about nutrition in general,
but it does seem odd that moderate alcohol consumption is
sometimes singled out for having modest effects on cancer
risk when it has always been a part of human diets. The recent ubiquity of processed foods in our diets correlates much
better with increases in degenerative diseases.[3]

Looking beyond simply the amount of alcohol consumed is essential, even for alcohol-related ill-health. It is
well known that socio-economic group affects the burden of
alcohol-related disease. Professional groups drink more than
lower income groups yet lower income groups are at least
3 times more likely to suffer an alcohol-related death.[4] It is
not altogether clear why this is the case, but a healthier diet
overall must be a possible contributor.

I believe the evidence shows that you can drink in moderation without worrying that you are doing yourself harm.
On the other hand, although there are modest benefits from
drinking, I do not think they should be overstated in isolation; moderate drinking is only one aspect of a healthy lifestyle. In a book entitled "The Wine Diet", Professor Corder

---

3   Erasmus U. Fats that heal, fats that kill. Alive books. 1993 Chs 2,6

4   UK House of Commons Health Committee. Alcohol, first report of session
2009-10. 8 January 2010 pp26, 112-3

extols the virtues of red wine.[5] But despite the appealing title
of the book, the author is only recommending drinking as
part of a much broader approach to healthy eating.

After conducting the research for this book, my views
are quite simple. On the balance of evidence to-date, moderate drinkers of all alcoholic beverages benefit overall and in
particular from a reduction in cardiovascular disease as they
get older. Beverages containing high levels of polyphenolic
compounds probably give additional benefits above alcohol
alone, putting red wine on the top step of the medal rostrum.
Regular heavy drinking and binge drinking are not clever.
Drinkers, particularly younger drinkers, should be aware of
the acute effects of alcohol on injury and violence; but that
is a separate issue from the health effects of regular alcohol
consumption. I suspect that some of the positive and negative consequences of alcohol on health will be shown to be
smaller, or non-existent, than they are currently thought to be
as other factors affecting health are better understood.

I did not set out to 'discover' how to deal with the
genuine alcohol problems, be it young binge drinkers or
confirmed alcoholics who are pickling their livers. Some of
these issues are very serious and, I suspect, not easily solved.
I set out to see whether sensible folk could enjoy drinking in
moderation without feeling guilty that they may be damaging
their health. I believe they can.

Of course we have to define 'moderate drinking'.
Around the world, governments set limits for alcohol
consumption considered 'safe', 'low-risk' or 'moderate'. In
most countries, guidelines for women are lower than for

---

5   Corder R. The Wine Diet. Sphere. 2008.

men. Based on data published by the International Center for Alcohol Policies,[6] the majority of recommended limits for men lie between 2½ and 5 UK standard drinks per day; for women most limits are in a range from a little less than 2 to 5 UK standard drinks per day. The UK Government recommends no more than 2-3 standard drinks a day for women and 3-4 for men. Guidelines should not be set in stone but these do not seem unreasonable based on the available research, although one could argue that governments probably err on the cautious side. In any case, these guidelines are averages; smaller people should probably drink less, bigger, fit people can probably drink more as they have more body water through which to disperse the alcohol. However, if you accurately assess how much you are drinking you can probably consume one and a half times these limits and still be within the 'spirit' of the guidelines as most research is based on self-reported drinking that is significantly less than what people really drink. Finally, if you are careful about avoiding accidents and violence, there may well be even more leeway in the drinking guidelines.

Although these factors make it difficult to prescribe a precise cut-off for moderate drinking, they provide some basis for individuals to decide how much it is sensible to drink. For example, supposing you like to drink wine with your meal each evening, if you share a bottle with two other drinkers, it would be difficult for anyone to accuse you of drinking excessively.

If you share a bottle with your spouse or partner, you may be getting near the limit, particularly if is a bottle of

---

Australian shiraz at 14% ABV. Yet even here, if the men are slightly more generous when filling their own glasses than when filling the glasses of their wives or girlfriends, the alcohol intake could be around 6 units for the men and 4 for the women. Allowing for the underreporting factor in alcohol research, that probably is just about within the spirit of the current UK Government guidelines of 3-4 units for men and 2-3 for women. You might, however, wish to skip the aperitif and the glass of brandy or port after the meal.

On the other hand, if the only person with whom you are sharing the bottle of wine is yourself, you might want to seek some help!

Probably more important than the guidelines themselves is knowing, reasonably accurately, how much you are drinking on a regular basis. Armed with that knowledge and some common sense, I suspect most people are well on the way to drinking healthily.

If I had to sum up a sensible approach to alcohol consumption, I suspect five words of advice would be sufficient: drink, but don't get drunk.

If that is too fastidious for you, try: drink, but don't get drunk (at least not often).

Appendix

ACCESSING RESEARCH ON THE
EFFECTS OF CONSUMING ALCOHOL

Throughout this book, a number of papers and reports are referenced in the footnotes. This appendix is provided as a brief guide on how to read cited papers and reports or to access other related research. Indeed, for those that wish to look more deeply into the subject, most of the papers cited in this book contain further long lists of references to relevant research. Consequently, even starting with just a handful of research papers can broaden out your research into a number of related areas. Of course, more topic-specific research can be done by performing internet searches on key words.

FINDING REPORTS

There are many ways of finding reports depending on the library and other facilities available to you, some of which may have staff that can assist in tracking down specific material. However, much can also be done using the internet.

Most government papers can be found by first locating the appropriate department or government agency's website and then entering the title of the required report in the search facility for that website.

For example, to find the report cited in footnote 3 of chapter 2: "UK Department of Health. Safe. Sensible. Social. The next steps in the National Alcohol Strategy. 5 June 2007: p16", first search for the UK Department of Health website and then enter 'safe sensible social' in the search facility. That should bring up the report.

Similarly, to find the report at footnote 6 of chapter 2: "World Health Organization. Global Status Report on Alcohol 2004: p41", first find the World Health Organization website and then enter 'global status report alcohol 2004' in the search facility.

Sometimes it may take a few search variations to find what you want, but usually it is fairly straight forward. A few footnotes give actual website addresses. They are obviously easy to find if the material has not been moved since the time of writing this book. If it has moved, where possible, searching within the relevant website may track down the material.

FINDING SPECIFIC RESEARCH PAPERS

Again, the ease with which you can find specific research papers will depend on the resources available to you. First of all, it is important to understand what the citations mean. Generally, papers are referred to in a fairly uniform way. Take for example, the paper referred to at footnote 2 in chapter 2: "Di Castelnuovo A, Costanzo S, Bagnardi V, Donati M, Iacoviello L, de Gaetano G. Alcohol dosing and total mortality in men and women: an updated meta-analysis of 34 prospective studies. Archives of Internal Medicine. 11-25 Dec 2006; 166(22):2437-45.".

The first part of the citation is the name(s) of the author or authors; usually the first author's name is sufficient, ie 'Di Castelnuovo'.

The second piece of information is the paper's title, here: 'Alcohol dosing and total mortality in men and women: an updated meta-analysis of 34 prospective studies'.

Next comes the name of the journal, here: 'Archives of Internal Medicine'.

Next comes the year or possibly a more specific date for the publication of the paper, or the date range that the journal covers, here '11-25 Dec 2006'.

Finally, the journal volume, journal issue and journal starting page number (or range of page numbers) is given. Here, the paper can be found in volume 166, issue 22, pages 2437 to 2445.

Depending on how you are accessing a particular paper, any or all of these pieces of information will be useful; if you are using a journal search facility, just enter the bits of information for which you are asked. Typically, you will want to find the relevant journal first and then search for the specific paper.

If you are searching on the internet, find the journal's website first, next find the relevant issue of the journal by using the volume, issue and date information. Finally, track down the article by page number or author/title.

One particularly useful search engine that is available directly over the internet is www.pubmed.com. This US database contains information on millions of biomedical research papers, with abstracts for many and often with links to the full text of the paper.

To get started, if you enter in the search box the name of an author or two and one or two keywords from the title of the paper, you can often find a paper very quickly. Using the earlier example, enter: 'di castelnuovo[AU] AND alcohol[TI] AND mortality[TI]' and you will soon find the paper. The letters in square brackets after search words refer to 'author' and 'title' respectively. The 'ANDs' simply make the search engine look for all the search words together for the same paper. Searches can be refined further and there is plenty of information provided on the www.pubmed.com website on how to search.

Of course, if you cannot get direct links to the papers you want, you need to find a suitable library. If your local library does not stock the journals you are interested in it may be possible to get access to national libraries or university libraries. For example, in the UK it is possible to order material from the British Library through a local library.

SPECIFIC SUBJECT SEARCHES

Using www.pubmed.com you can perform quite specific searches on a particular topic. For example, if you are interested in looking in depth at the link between breast cancer and alcohol, type 'breast[TI] AND cancer[TI] AND alcohol[TI]' into the search engine and it will bring up dozens of papers with those terms in the title. If you wish to be more specific, there are more advanced search facilities too. For example, you could narrow the search results down to articles that have only been published in the last 3 years – just click on 'Limits' (above the main search field) to see some of the options.

Index

Lightning Source UK Ltd.
Milton Keynes UK
25 October 2010

161843UK00011B/58/P